"I have seen firsthand how Payal's goal setting methodology helps set short-term goals for long-lasting results. Here, she has shared a path for an honest, fulfilling, and meaningful existence. Read this book and change your life. Honestly."

—JESSICA ALBA

"With ClassPass, Payal paved the way to discovering the best versions of ourselves. With *LifePass*, she is doing the same—helping us to pursue our passions without constraints, and live with new strength and tenacity."

—RANDI ZUCKERBERG

"Everyone is always searching for the one secret formula for success, but in reality it's such a personal journey. *LifePass* is a master class on how to live the life you've always wanted and thrive."

—ARIANNA HUFFINGTON

A GROUNDBREAKING APPROACH TO GOAL SETTING

LIFEPASS

DROP YOUR LIMITS
RISE TO YOUR POTENTIAL

PAYAL KADAKIA

FOUNDER OF **classpass**

CHRONICLE PRISM

Library of Congress Cataloging-in-Publication Data available.

ISBN 978-1-7972-0694-3

Manufactured in the United States of America.

Design by Brooke Johnson.
Typesetting by Maureen Forys, Happenstance Type-O-Rama.
Typeset in Mercury Text, Knockout, and TT Norms.

10 9 8 7 6 5 4 3 2 1

Chronicle books and gifts are available at special quantity discounts to corporations, professional associations, literacy programs, and other organizations. For details and discount information, please contact our premiums department at corporatesales@chroniclebooks.com or at 1-800-759-0190.

♋ CHRONICLE PRISM

Chronicle Prism is an imprint of Chronicle Books LLC, 680 Second Street, San Francisco, California 94107

www.chronicleprism.com

THIS BOOK IS DEDICATED TO

My parents, Geeta & Harshad, who gave me life.

My husband, Nick, who brings love to my life.

My son, Zayn, who let me create life.

contents

Introduction I

PART I
YOUR LIFE

1
CALLING
What drives you?
9

2
IDENTITY
What makes you stand out?
27

3
EXPECTATIONS
Whose life are you living?
45

4
FEAR
What is stopping you?
63

PART 2

YOUR LIMITS

5
FINANCES
What is money worth to you?
83

6
SKILLS
What do you bring to the table?
101

7
PEOPLE
Who will aid you on your journey?
117

8
TIME
*How are you investing
your most valuable asset?*
135

PART 3

YOUR LIFEPASS

9
THE LIFEPASS METHOD
Reflect
How would you describe
your past year?

Dream
Where do you want to go?

Focus
What are your priorities?

Set Goals
What's your plan?
159

Afterword   217

Acknowledgments   221

About the Author   224

INTRODUCTION

A LITTLE OVER A DECADE AGO, I started the company ClassPass, a fitness and wellness membership that allows members to book classes and experiences online. What most people don't know is that my original vision for ClassPass was for it to be a LifePass—a way to connect to soul-nurturing experiences, fitness, and beyond.

While ClassPass has soared to millions of reservations across the globe, ClassPass is not just about classes. It is about keeping our passions alive and continuing to discover and evolve even as we get older. "Every life, fully lived" is our vision statement. It's a way for each person to do the most with the hours of their day, a message this book similarly aims to impart.

LifePass shares my philosophy and offers a guide for living a fulfilled life. People frequently ask me how I was able to craft a career and life out of the things I loved. The answer is always the same: a lot of self-reflection and planning!

It took hard work, but it was worth it. And more so, I believe the methodology I've created can be used by anyone to unleash a life of fulfillment, joy, and purpose. I wrote this book to share it with you. In *LifePass*, I walk you through the step-by-step process I used so you can do it yourself. If I were sitting with you, these are the questions I'd ask and the steps I'd tell you to take.

In conversations and collaborations with incredible entrepreneurs and creators in my own journey, as well as through developing a goal-setting process and sharing it with others, I've discovered that there are common things that hold people back. I frequently hear people saying things like, "I can't do what I love because I don't have enough money or time," or "I didn't know the right people," or "I don't pursue my dream because I lacked a certain skill." Even deeper than this are the internal limits of not knowing what drives us, feeling like we don't fit in, the expectations of others, and of course, the fear of failure that can prevent us from even getting started.

I have faced and often still face all of these gating factors. But I have found a way to work through these constraints. Instead of feeling that I can't do what I love because of obstacles, I've learned to break through those barriers to accomplish what I want. I've found a way to live free of limits, and my hope is to help others develop that mindset as well.

To do this, we need new tools and a new way of thinking. Many constraints, as well as our experiences, can shape the way we think, but it's possible to work through the limits that exist in our minds. This involves asking deep questions about our past and examining any difficult times to identify what may be standing in our way. Once we do this, we can develop a plan for moving forward and going after our dreams. Having a plan is like donning a parachute before jumping out of an airplane. In this book, we will build your parachute so that you can safely, securely, and confidently take the leap you've always wanted.

Life is full of practical considerations. We need to pay bills and take care of our responsibilities to family, work, and so on. But that does not mean that we can't also go for what we want in our lives. By shifting our perceptions and developing a plan, we can approach apparent limits and constraints so these things work for us instead of against us.

Part 1 focuses on shifting perceptions by identifying the ways we might be mentally hindering our journey. This starts with identifying and clarifying our calling. I discuss how to find it and follow it, and the importance of protecting it. Next, I discuss identity and expectations. How we see ourselves and the expectations others set might also be getting in the way, but we can shift both of these things to improve our efforts and foster success. Lastly, I discuss fear and self-doubt, and how to embrace our emotions so that we always keep moving forward.

Part 2 focuses on four common issues everyone must deal with: money, personal skills, other people, and time. People often experience each of these as constraints. But we can shift our relationships and current patterns within each area to break through these seeming barriers and turn them into opportunity.

Throughout, I illustrate these lessons by sharing my own personal story, but my main goal is for you to pause and reflect on your own wants, needs, patterns, and life. To kick-start this, each chapter includes Self-Check Points with questions and exercises, and as you read, you may want to have a notebook and pen handy (or a computer or phone to take notes on) so you can pause and write down your thoughts in the moment. Each chapter also ends with a mantra for you to internalize and carry forward.

Part 3 takes you through the LifePass Method, the goal-setting process that I created during one of the hardest times in my life, when many things seemed to be falling apart. I found that I needed a system to help me achieve what I wanted out of life, both professionally and personally. This planning method has enabled me to achieve many of my dreams while ensuring I stay true to myself and what I want. This includes building and growing a family, leading ClassPass to extraordinary heights, continuing with my passion for Indian dance, staying intellectually inspired, building a sense of "home" in a new city, remaining connected to those I deeply care about, and much more.

None of this happened overnight and without plenty of hiccups along the way. And of course, my life has also been blessed in many ways, not least of which by my parents, who are very supportive. However, ultimately, we are in charge of our own lives. By reflecting on myself, refining this process over time, and following it diligently, I have been able to work toward my goals while continually pushing myself and growing in new areas. I have gained confidence from knowing that *I* can decide what I want, and no matter my circumstances, I can use this method to reevaluate and achieve it, creating a fulfilling life based on my own priorities and my own definition of success and happiness.

My hope is that this book will help you do the same thing. This method can help you identify what you want out of life, set priorities and goals that reflect who you want to be, and provide you with a concrete plan to get there.

How are you living your life? How do you want to be living it?

PART I

YOUR
LIFE

1

CALLING

What drives you?

IT'S IRONIC THAT THE MOMENT that really launched my life, the exact situation that allowed it to take off, was also one of the lowest moments of my career.

I was working at Bain & Company, a prestigious management consulting firm in New York City, because it seemed like what I was "supposed" to do. When I graduated from MIT in 2005, all of my friends were going into banking or consulting, so I followed suit and applied to those types of jobs as well. When I landed a coveted position that would make my parents proud and look good on my resume, I didn't give it much thought beyond that.

For two and a half years, I worked hard as an associate consultant. I wanted to do well, get promoted, and rise in the ranks. Then six months before my contract was up for renewal, I was sitting in my manager's office and, for the first time ever, receiving negative feedback.

"I have to question your reliability and commitment to your clients," my manager plainly told me, sitting behind her desk. "If you really want to further your career as a consultant, your clients are going to have to come first. I don't know if that's the case for you."

Even though my manager didn't say it, I knew deep down what she was referring to. In addition to working seventy to eighty hours a week at my consulting job, I was also studying dance, which I had done for most of my life, and performing with a troupe called Bollywood Axion. I spent my nights and weekends rehearsing with the troupe, and about six months before, a big performance had been scheduled on the same day as an important client meeting. I had a visceral reaction when I discovered the conflict. While it felt irresponsible to consider missing the meeting—attendance was typically mandatory— every fiber of my being told me I *had* to be at the show. There had always been limited opportunities for Indian dancers to perform, and I couldn't stand the idea of not participating. Plus, this show was to celebrate the opening of a Bollywood exhibit at Madame Tussauds featuring Aishwarya Rai, a huge Bollywood film star I had always admired. I wanted to be a part of it!

I made up my mind that I would go to the event and simply tell my boss that I would miss the meeting. I decided to play it straight, no excuses. I explained that I had a personal dance commitment I had to attend. I added that I wasn't critical to the work meeting, since I wouldn't be presenting or interacting directly with the client.

My manager didn't make a big deal about it at the time. In fact, I thought our discussion went well, and the performance went even better. But now, half a year later, I was paying the price. It *had* impacted the way my boss saw me and may have made a dent in my career trajectory. I was devastated.

My whole life, I had lived by the book and worked hard to excel at everything. Now it felt like I was being punished for doing what I loved, for falling out of line just once, and I feared my career might suffer as a result. After completing a three-year contract at Bain, most associate consultants went to business school with an offer to return to Bain, while a select few were offered the opportunity to stay on as a consultant without going to business school. Up to then, I thought I was doing well enough that both were potential options, but for the first time, I started to think about what would happen if I didn't remain at Bain. Several of my friends were taking the GMATs and applying to business school. I had bought study guides for the test but never opened them and never registered for the exam. While business school might have been something to pursue down the road, I knew I didn't want to go right then. But after my shaky review, was the offer of a full consultant position even going to be an option?

My initial instinct was to dive fully back into work and prove to my boss that I was worthy of staying on as a consultant. But as I worked harder to prove myself, I realized that this effort would only require *more* hours, *increased* travel, and *far less* time for dance, which is what I truly loved doing. This forced me to consider whether becoming a consultant was what I even wanted. I had been set on staying "top bucket" at Bain, but as I thought about what that commitment really meant, I knew it wasn't my dream job.

I sat with this for a few months during my "externship" with Bain; this is a program that allows you to work in another company and industry for six months. In my temporary post at MTV, I had a little more space to think, and I saw that other career options would give me more time for dance. As I fantasized about leaving work at five or six each night instead of ten, and of being able to dance in the evenings *and* still have enough time to sleep, I realized my boss was completely right. I *wasn't* fully committed to being a consultant. I wasn't making Bain my everything, because it simply wasn't enough for me.

My manager wasn't being harsh in that review. In fact, she was mentoring me. She helped me ask myself some hard questions that put me on the right path. Many people stay at their jobs for years, doing what they feel they are supposed to, without ever asking themselves the hard questions about what they really want. Up until that point in my life, I had made most of my decisions based on what I thought I should do. I performed well in high school in order to get into one of a handful of acceptable colleges, after which I thought my career options amounted to working at either one of the three top consulting firms or the three top banks. This view was so limited, and so wrong! There was a world of options—but I didn't see them because I was following someone else's path. I only knew how to succeed by following what was laid out for me. Now, I realized, it was time to chart my own journey.

I finally understood why I had reacted so strongly to that negative review. It stemmed from my own insecurities and desire for external validation. A guaranteed offer to be a consultant wasn't my life's goal, or even how I wanted to devote my time. What I wanted was more time to create, dance, and serve others. I wanted the ability to pursue what fulfilled me. I had to find a way to be responsible, make money, and keep moving forward professionally while also opening up more time to pursue my calling. I knew I needed to learn to protect what I loved. No one else was going to do that for me.

FIND YOUR GIFT AND GIVE IT AWAY

One of my favorite quotes is now the mantra that I live by. It has been attributed to both William Shakespeare and Pablo Picasso: "The meaning of life is to find your gift. The purpose is to give it away." In other words: Your calling is a passion that exists both for yourself and for the benefit of others. In order for this calling to exist, you must first discover it and then prioritize it.

This is what I hope the example of my story and this book will help you to do. Perhaps you have already had an "aha moment" about your calling or perhaps not. Many people don't discover their calling until later in life. The good news is that it's never too late.

> *Everyone must come to their own*
> *realization in their own way and follow their*
> *own path. We can't follow someone else's blueprint.*
> *Our answer lies within us.*

I define a calling this way: It is the action we take to fulfill our purpose in life, what we were put on this planet to do and share with the world. The passion for our calling provides the fuel to power us through the inevitable roadblocks that appear. Our calling is what makes life feel worthwhile and helps us reach our highest potential. It is the direction of our true north.

Take a moment to think about what your calling might be and the expectations that others have for you or that you feel have been piled on you. Many people mistake their calling for something their parents told them to pursue or something that is valued by our society. But a true calling isn't an obligation or responsibility.

It isn't pursued to please someone else. It also isn't something we simply enjoy or even excel at; it's not always the easiest path to take. A calling reflects our passion. We feel a magnetic connection to it that serves as our vehicle for giving to others, and that can only be defined by ourselves. This is often the hardest part!

Once I realized that management consulting was not my calling, I had to decide what I did want to do. *How did I want to spend my time? What did I want to do with my life?* I had never asked myself that before.

I reflected on my connection to dance, something I loved. I knew that dancing was more than a hobby, but I had never been able to pour all of my energy into it due to a handful of different constraints, from not having enough time or money to society's expectations and my own doubts. A big part of me wondered what would happen if I started to think about it differently, especially because this sense of inspiration and wonder started for me when I was just a small child.

I grew up in the 1980s in a suburban New Jersey town where all the other kids were busy playing with Barbies and watching *Sesame Street*. I wasn't interested. Those dolls looked nothing like me and our TV only played the latest Bollywood films on VHS. I was obsessed with the dances in these movies and watched them over and over. I loved to see the emotive women and their intricate dance steps. Each time I rewatched those videos, I memorized the actresses' every expression and gesture, and then I spent hours replicating them in the mirror.

My parents had immigrated to the United States from India before I was born. They came for education and work, and later sponsored many family members who followed them in search of better opportunities. We often had aunties and uncles staying with us until they found a place of their own. One of those aunties was Tiku Bhabhi, my cousin's wife. At twenty-one, she was youthful and full of energy, also loved Bollywood films, and looked like me—something I appreciated, since I didn't look like any of the other kids in my neighborhood. I adored being around her and connecting to where I came from.

When I was five years old, Tiku Bhabhi noticed me dancing along to a movie in our living room and trying my best to imitate the expressions of the woman on the screen. The actress was lovingly mocking her boyfriend and dancing in a lighthearted way to the rhythm of an upbeat, fast-paced song. My Bhabhi, dressed in a T-shirt and pants, stood confidently in front of the TV and told me to copy her as she came alive dancing like the women on the small screen. Over the next hour, she broke down all of the dance moves, showing me exactly how to hold my arms and tilt my head to look more like the actress I admired.

The next day, my whole family got dressed up and went to a huge banquet hall. I don't remember if it was a wedding or a holiday or a birthday celebration; these events, with hundreds of people from the Indian community, were regular fixtures in my life. Ever since I could walk, I spent the majority of my weekends running around a backyard or outdoor catering venue with dozens of other girls in fancy, embroidered lehenga cholis, arms full of colorful bangles.

At first, this party was no different. But after a little while, the song my Tiku Bhabhi and I had been dancing to, "Kabhi Tu Chhalia Lagta Hai," came on over the speakers. Without really thinking about it, I walked up to the dance floor and started performing the way she'd taught me. The familiar melody struck a chord within me, and I remember being lost in the music and movements, placing my hand on my chin and moving my head from side to side like a little doll in tempo to the song.

Before I knew what was happening, the large crowd on the dance floor had gathered to watch me as they clapped and cheered with huge smiles on their faces. That night, on the dance floor, I could see that my performance made people happy. That made me feel overcome with joy.

Looking back, I recognize this as the moment I realized on a deep, intuitive level that I could use dance, something I was passionate about, as a vehicle to move other people. I didn't understand it this way at the time, but performing became one of my callings—a way of using my passion to fulfill a need in the world.

However, just because I found my calling early on didn't mean that my path was set. We may love something or identify a calling as children, but instead of following that dream into adulthood, we often end up doing what we see as the responsible thing, the mature thing, or what others expect. My adult life started no differently.

WHAT DRIVES YOU? | SELF-CHECK POINT

We have all experienced moments of pure joy when we are doing something we love so much that we feel completely fulfilled just from doing it. Childhood can be filled with such moments, when we are encouraged to try new things, explore, and *play*.

Yet as adults, we can let the things we love fall by the wayside. They can get replaced by responsibilities and obligations and the constraints of societal norms: We get married, have kids, get a promotion, and no longer have time to do anything "just for fun." But it's critical not to lose our sense of playful joy.

We must continue to have these types of moments, which give us more than just joy—they call us powerfully toward our purpose.

To reconnect to your playful side, think of an activity that you truly care about and that energizes you. Go back as far as you need to—all the way back to childhood, if necessary. What matters is that these activities and feelings have no ulterior motive. The activity isn't about chasing acknowledgment, money, or fame. Pinpoint something you love to do for its own sake, whether or not you get paid or someone gives you a pat on the back.

To identify your calling, think about the activities you have felt the most passionate about throughout your life, and the ones that have allowed you to give something meaningful to others. Take a moment to meditate on what you care about, and write down your answers to the following questions:

1   What activities were you most passionate about when you were younger?

2   When do you feel or when have you felt the most alive?

3   What causes and issues in the world do you feel passionate about today?

Review your answers. Your calling in life, whether you know it or not, is most likely connected to one or more of them. For additional perspective, ask your closest friends what they think you truly love. Sometimes, we don't even realize how much we enjoy something, or we block out this knowledge because we're afraid of disappointing others or being judged. When someone who knows us well tells us about the times that they've seen us light up, we may gain fresh insight about our truest desires.

YOUR CALLING WILL REVEAL ITSELF

There is a Buddhist saying that when the student is ready, the teacher will appear, and the same is true of your calling. *Listen closely, and your calling will reveal itself to you.* As you're tuning in to yourself, and along this entire journey, make sure to open up space and time for your thoughts. If your mind is constantly busy and occupied, you won't be able to hear the sound of your inner voice. I know this from my own experience. I was so busy following what I thought I should be doing that I almost didn't hear that voice.

When my contract was up at Bain, I found a job in 2008 working on licensing agreements for digital music at Warner Music Group. It paid less and wasn't as prestigious, and most of the people in my life looked at me as if I were a little bit crazy. Why would I switch gears like that? Although I didn't admit this at the time, it was a "half step," or a compromise that felt most comfortable at that moment. I wasn't quitting my job to dance full-time, but I was giving myself more predictable hours. I still had a steady income, but instead of chasing the golden goose, I was prioritizing my own wants and needs and looked forward to having a workday end at 5 p.m. so I could attend dance classes and rehearsals in the evening.

I was in a state of transition. The same week I started my new job I also decided to leave Bollywood Axion. I had started to choreograph my own dance pieces—something I poured all of my emotions into and found to be a powerful way to express myself. Though it started organically, this ultimately led me to start a dance company. There were so few artistic spaces to represent Indian culture on the stage. I wanted to create a new way of showcasing Indian dance beyond merely as a form of entertainment or fun. I was inspired by dance companies like Alvin Ailey, the New York City Ballet, Stephen Petronio, and others, which performed at some of the most prestigious performing arts venues in the city, from the Joyce Theater to Lincoln Center. I knew how meaningful it would be for an Indian audience to see our culture being celebrated and elevated in a similar way, and I wanted to offer them that experience. I also hoped that a new representation of the Indian American identity would help those living with dual identities—something I struggled with—feel more whole.

With more time on my hands, I approached some of the best dancers I knew and asked if they wanted to work together on some choreography. Some of these dancers were from the Bollywood Axion group, some I had danced with at MIT, and others I'd known since we were little girls learning dances in our basements. I named our group the Sa Dance Company (named for the first and last note in the Indian octave, "Sa")—our own dance company to tell our own story.

Shortly after starting Sa, I applied for us to participate in an annual Indian dance festival in downtown Manhattan. We weren't an obvious fit, as this festival tended to showcase prestigious classical Indian dancers and companies, but after a lot of emails, coffee chats, and discussions with the dance curator, Prachi, she took me under her wing and decided to give us a chance. The festival was a blast, and it was enthralling to perform to a full audience outdoors among NYC's skyscrapers. The Friday night after the festival, Prachi called me. The performance hadn't gone exactly as planned; we had initially discussed doing a traditional type of Indian folk dance, but with her guidance we decided to also include a number with a more contemporary flair. I thought she was going to give me constructive criticism on the performance, so I braced myself. I thought, *Maybe she got into trouble for allowing that? Maybe it was too unorthodox? Maybe we weren't good enough.* As my mind raced with the doomsday possibilities, she explained that Alastair Macaulay, the renowned *New York Times* dance critic, was featuring the festival in the next day's Arts section. "And guess what? Sa is going to be on the cover."

I will never forget getting the *Times* first thing on Saturday morning and opening it to see the Arts section with a huge half-page image of Sa in midmotion. The dancers looked radiant. I was so proud. It felt like a sign that I was on the right track.

That Monday, when I went to work at Warner Music Group, everyone had seen the photo and article, and it gave them a new understanding of who I was—my full self, not just the person who showed up to the office every day. My boss came to my office early that morning and said, "I saw you and your company in the paper yesterday. Honestly, I didn't think we were going to see you in the office!" I could tell that he didn't mean just that day, but had actually wondered if I'd ever show up again.

It felt like the universe was telling me to believe in myself and what I was doing. It sounds cheesy, but my calling was calling! I tossed my GMAT books that were collecting dust in my apartment, almost like a physical representation of my backup plan.

I spent the next several months showing up for work and planning Sa's weekend-long Premiere NYC Showcase. Inspired by the response to our performance at the festival, I dove into making my own production, writing my own story, creating new choreography, and rehearsing for hours with the dancers, with the goal of sharing the beauty of Indian dance. I was excited to invite my colleagues, and I was grateful that many of them showed up at the performance to support me.

Back at work on Monday after the event, the head of my group, Michael Nash, brought me a gift—an anthology of Bollywood dance. Sitting at my desk, I was flipping through the book of celebrated choreographers and dancers when I stopped on a page. I was shocked to find an article about the dance troupe MIT Chamak, which I had started in college. There in that book of artists that I had looked up to since I was a toddler was my very own name.

Sitting in that office, leafing through that book, I began to gain clarity. When I took the job at Warner two years earlier, I knew it wasn't my passion. But I was good at it, it paid the bills, and it signified to the outside world that I was a responsible adult in all the expected ways. But there was still a disconnect between the person I was at work and the life I wanted for myself.

I asked myself: *Why are you shutting this part of you off during the day? Why do you think you have no choice but to stay in a corporate job?*

For the first time, I considered a future without my day job and where I could blend the business, creative, and entrepreneurial sides of me to make a real impact on the world. I sensed that the only way to fully stitch together my various identities and make the kind of difference I wanted was to start living life on my own terms. For me, that meant creating something on my own.

TO IGNITE INSPIRATION, TRY SOMETHING NEW

During this period, I spent nearly all my time working and dancing and didn't do much else. I shut almost everything else out, including drinks with friends and travel. Then, in the summer of 2010, one of my closest friends, Parul, invited me to San Francisco for her birthday. On a whim, I decided to go, and the trip became a life-altering lesson in how getting a change of pace and gaining some distance can sometimes be exactly what we need to gain perspective.

Parul had just moved to the West Coast with her husband and settled into her new life pretty quickly. As soon as I arrived in California, I was swept right into the birthday gathering and spent the night chatting with her friends, all of whom seemed to be developing apps, starting companies, or embarking on some type of entrepreneurial journey. I was completely enamored with the fact that these people were pursuing exciting, creative projects as an actual career path. They were unlike anyone I knew in New York, where my business friends were consumed with their jobs, and my dance friends relied on side hustles to pay their bills while they pursued their dreams. I was sort of stuck in the middle, working a job that didn't fulfill me while relegating my calling to second place.

A few days later, on Sunday night, I couldn't sleep on the red-eye flight back to New York. My mind was racing with inspiration. The idea of creating something on my own as my career, and not just a side hustle, fascinated me, and I wondered how I could start something that would provide the same type of freedom and inspiration. I wanted to be like Parul's friends, people who spent their days working on something they owned and cared about deeply.

Before I landed, I set myself a goal. I had two weeks to come up with an idea for something I would be passionate about creating. I knew that if I focused my mind, I could potentially get to an answer. If I didn't, then maybe this wasn't the right path for me at the moment.

On Monday, because I was so tired from my trip, I didn't go to ballet class after work, something I typically did every day. On Tuesday morning, I packed up my ballet clothes and headed to my office, my mind whirling with ideas—*How could I improve my flying experience? What would it take to make my work commute better? Was there a way to take phone calls in the shower?* But nothing stuck. Just being in that creative mental space, though, inspired me to break out of my routine. I suddenly realized that I didn't want to take the same ballet class I had been taking. I was ready to push myself and try something more challenging.

After lunch, I opened my laptop and started looking for a new class. I searched the websites for different ballet studios across the city, comparing their schedules, researching their instructors, and mapping out their locations. Two hours later, I looked up. I had thirty open browser tabs and realized I had wasted much of the afternoon without finding anything.

I went home frustrated. I was a busy, tech-savvy person, and apps had solved many problems in my life. I ordered lunch every day through Seamless, made doctors' appointments through Zocdoc, and found new restaurants with OpenTable. Why wasn't there one place I could go to find and book classes?

That hindrance turned into my entrepreneurial epiphany. As a dancer, staying active and going to class was a daily requirement I was very familiar with. I also had fought to keep dance in my life for so long. To make time for it, I had given up high-profile work assignments, said no to countless social events, and at times, reduced sleep to the bare minimum. No one was more familiar with the obstacles that could keep one's passion from being present in everyday life than me. So if I was feeling frustrated by not being able to efficiently find and sign up for the right class, surely other people were, too. In fact, I knew I had to do something about it. This was the earliest inkling for ClassPass. As an app, it became a way to give people the opportunity to keep moving and try new things, and as a business, it became a new path for my life that aligned my calling with my career.

EXPLORE SOMETHING NEW | SELF-CHECK POINT

Trying something new can open doors to unknown parts of ourselves and our journey. The adrenaline rush of doing something new and exciting also builds confidence and creates beneficial changes in our brain. It can make us sharper and more creative and better at everything we do.

So seek new experiences and activities that reconnect you to your sense of wonder, and/or simply make changes to your everyday environment and even vary the people you spend time with. Then, don't stop exploring and trying new things. It's equally important to continue to switch things up, whether that means taking a new class, going somewhere different, or meeting new people. You never know what might spark a creative inspiration within. If you are unsure on where to begin, ask yourself these questions:

I **What things are you doing right now that you don't want to do?**

2 What new things have you tried lately, and how did you enjoy them?

3 What things haven't you tried but would like to?

As children do, explore without any expectations. Don't feel pressure to do things in order to find your calling. Rather, as much as you can, stop doing or minimize the things you are not excited about and perhaps only do out of obligation, and make more time for the things you truly enjoy. Prioritize exploration itself, and see where that leads you.

I strive to find and follow my unique purpose in this life.

2

IDENTITY

What makes you stand out?

WHEN I WAS IN THIRD GRADE and heard that my elementary school would be holding a talent show, I immediately signed up. Finally, the two sides of me—the grade-schooler who spent her weekdays trying to fit in with the white girls and the performer who spent her weekends practicing Indian dance—could come together.

On the day of the show, I stood on the stage of the elementary school auditorium in my blue and red chaniya choli and Indian bangles and necklaces. I had rehearsed the sequence so many times that, as the music began, my body moved without me even having to think about it. I was focused on the careful technique and steps—until I heard a noise over the music. It sounded like someone booing. I paused midgesture. There it was again. Then it got louder. Within seconds, the entire auditorium full of kids was booing and jeering. The wave of hatred drowned me. I ran off the stage and burst into tears.

For years, the girls at school had been making fun of me, saying I was ugly and smelled bad. Our school's playground had two separate blacktop areas to play on—the right side and the left side. One day at recess, all the girls were gathered on the right side, and when I tried to join them, they stopped me. "You can't come over here," one of the girls told me. "You're not one of us." Words and phrases like this can cause a wound so deep they leave a scar.

After the talent show humiliation, I begged my parents not to send me back to school. I thought that I would never fit in and was sick of the constant bullying. But of course, nine-year-old girls in suburban New Jersey are required to attend school, so I had no choice except to learn how to survive. My solution was not a good one: I created a divide that kept the American and Indian sides of my life completely separate.

In many ways, it worked. In school and with friends, hiding pieces of myself that would be seen as different kept me feeling safe. By the time I started high school, I was no longer ostracized by my classmates, and I quickly learned how arbitrary social status can be. My background in dance translated to something more relatable—cheerleading—and making the cheerleading squad made me feel accepted. I was the smallest girl, so I got to be the "flier" who did cool tricks. This came naturally, and I even managed to become somewhat popular. Performing at football games, I was able to access the same confidence that I possessed onstage, and the people who once looked down on me began to warm to me—at least, the parts that I shared with them.

I felt split between two dimensions. Sometimes it felt as if I had to choose between the two sides, whereas other times it felt like neither was strong enough. Around my Indian friends, I feared I would be perceived as "too American," and around my white friends, I was afraid of being exposed as not American enough.

So, life continued to be a life divided. My cheerleading and my American friends on one side, and my family, dance, and Indian friends on the other. This duality in my life was highlighted in the fall during football season, which coincided every year with the Hindu festival Navratri. This festival traditionally lasts nine nights, but since everyone in our community had to go to work and school during the week, we celebrated at a high school gym every Friday and Saturday night from 9 p.m. to 2 a.m. for four weekends straight.

Meanwhile, my high school was similar to the one in the TV show *Friday Night Lights*. We were a Division I school, and in football, this was a huge deal. Thousands of people attended. During my senior year, I became captain of our varsity cheerleading squad, and I was expected to be at every game. That meant that for four weekends I was supposed to be at two places at the same time: the high-pressure football games and the beautiful cultural experience with my community. That year, I couldn't choose between these two things that I loved, so I did the only thing I knew how: I split myself in two.

One Friday night of Navratri, the football game was turning into the biggest of the season. I looked at my watch nervously. We were winning, and there were only a few minutes left on the clock. I quickly did the math in my head. If I could change in less than ten minutes, I might still make it to Navratri in time for Garba, a flowy, circular dance that was my favorite part of the night. It was going to be tight.

As soon as the game ended, I congratulated the team and sprinted to my car to change in the back seat. As the crowd cheered in the distance, I swapped my cheerleading uniform for my elaborate Navratri outfit, trying to make sure that no one could see me. This was no easy feat. My ensemble consisted of a full top, bottom, and oddhini (a nine-foot-long Indian scarf) that draped around me and had to be pinned together in several places. Then I piled on jewelry—earrings, necklaces, and bangles in the same bright colors as my dress, and anklets, ironically called "payal" in Hindi, that would jingle when I danced.

Once my outfit was perfectly assembled, I scrambled into the front seat to do my makeup. Seeing myself in the rearview mirror, I was struck by how different I looked. The freshly scrubbed all-American cheerleading captain with the high ponytail was gone, replaced completely by her Indian alter ego.

Back then, I didn't know that each of these identities could bolster the other if I allowed them to coexist. I didn't realize that one side didn't take away from the other. I was afraid to let the strands overlap, but with time and experience I've learned that my strength lies in the unique combination of strands that make up no one but me. Everyone's identity is like a rope that's braided together. When our separate strands are woven into one, we become far more beautifully complex and stronger, with the strands reinforcing one another—strength in unity.

Only when we tie together all the things that make us who we are can we finally feel whole. We are all multifaceted, regardless of what culture or cultures we come from. Throughout my career, I have not only felt torn between being Indian and American, but also between being an artist and a businesswoman, a tech start-up founder and a wife and mother, and more. I am many other things! Now, each aspect of my identity blends to create a whole version of me.

WHAT MAKES YOU STAND OUT?

We all face adversity in one form or another. There are a million reasons someone could be perceived as different, as "other." Many people respond to the perception of others the same way I did, by compartmentalizing certain parts of their identity. This response is a survival mechanism, but achieving a fulfilling life is about more than surviving. The path to *thriving* and reaching our potential begins with being our full, authentic self instead of hiding any side of our identity.

Take a moment to meditate on the following questions. These prompt you to consider whether different people in your life might describe you in wildly contrasting ways and how those descriptions compare to who you feel you are.

1 How do you characterize your own identity?

2 What are ways family members would identify you?

3 What are ways a close friend would identify you?

4 What are ways your boss and work colleagues would identify you?

Your answers to these questions can help you see how much of your full self you are bringing to the world in the different aspects of your life. If who you are differs drastically depending on who you are with, consider finding ways you can bring your whole self to all environments.

FIND YOUR HOME BASE

Growing up, I was always excited when September came—not because I would go back to school but because it started a countdown to the monthlong Navratri festival. This was the one time during the year when I could connect to my culture and feel normal. As a young child, I danced and ran around the hallways with little girls who looked like me; as I got older, I met friends with parents and aunties and uncles who looked like mine. It was heartwarming to see my parents light up when they were around their community. As a child of immigrants, I often witnessed my parents feeling uncomfortable. Like me, they also didn't fit in where we lived. Unlike a lot of the moms in town, my mother worked. Leaving for her job in the afternoon, coming home to put us to bed, and then going back to work until 2 or 3 a.m., she didn't have time to do the things other moms did. She didn't participate in the PTA or plan play dates. My parents had accents and didn't understand American etiquette. We socialized with other Indian people. My parents felt more at ease with those who had also left everything they knew to come here. People who understood the sacrifices they had made and were making.

Just as having a connection to their community helped them, it also saved me. Being able to see my Indian friends at festivals, family gatherings, cultural events, and through dance practice allowed me to express myself freely. When we are around the people who make us feel comfortable, our real selves will emerge.

I am a strong advocate for intentionally seeking out communities that reinforce the essential parts of our identity. And if you are seeking or wanting a community that does not exist, *create it*. For instance, dance has always been a big part of who I am. That's why every time I've moved, the first thing I've done is seek out a community of dancers. When I arrived at college at MIT, there was no Indian dance group on campus that specialized in my style of dance. At first, I traveled across the Charles River to Boston University to join the dancers there. Later, I created a dance troupe at MIT. When I moved to New York, I immediately found Bollywood Axion, and later I built Sa Dance Company. When I moved to LA, I worked hard to expand Sa and connect with the dance community on the West Coast. Always having this home base allowed the rest of me to flourish outside the dance studio.

This was also part of the mission of ClassPass—to help people find their home base. I wanted ClassPass to enable people to connect through an activity they shared—rather than through their profession, education, social group, or any of the labels we are given. Instead, ClassPass gave users an opportunity to be part of a group that shared similar interests. When people unite around a common focus, other differences often become irrelevant.

If you're struggling with fully sharing your identity, it's important to spend more time with the people who help you feel authentically yourself. They will reinforce who you are and help you build confidence in being you. Think about the following questions: *Who is your current home base? If you don't have one now, what was it in the past? What other or new communities could you seek out or create to foster your authentic self?*

REVEL IN YOUR ROOTS

Indian culture includes the concept of the "guru." This is someone whom we have so much respect and gratitude for that we touch their feet for blessings, we aim to never disappoint them, and we bring our best self whenever we are around them. It's considered a sacred relationship, since the guru is someone who shares their knowledge and wisdom with us—the greatest gift in the world.

Unlikely as it sounds, I found my guru in a New Jersey basement. By profession, Usha Aunty worked in finance at New York Life. In my childhood, she was everything.

Usha Aunty was one of my mom's best friends and a second mom to me—my dance mom. She spent her days working, cooking, and cleaning, but she spent her evenings and weekends as a volunteer teaching me—and sixty other young girls—to dance.

If you are imagining a friendly and encouraging teacher, think again. We were all terrified of her. She demanded we show up on time and always give our all. Although I wasn't the best dancer or even in the front row, I always tried my hardest. I didn't want to get yelled at for not practicing or be on the receiving end of her side-eye. In striving to please her, I found the best version of myself, but that is not why I consider her my guru. The knowledge she shared and the confidence she fostered transformed the way I saw myself.

Usha Aunty taught groups of different levels. When I started, I was in the youngest group. We traveled around New Jersey and sometimes out of state to dance competitions. I spent a lot of time with the friends I danced with, as well as with the older girls. When I was with them, I felt like I truly belonged. The older girls in particular had a big impact on me. They were beautiful and poised and kind to the younger students. One of the things that struck me the most was how comfortable the older girls were in their own skin. They never seemed to struggle with their identities the way I did with mine. They wore their differences with a sense of pride, which I greatly admired and strived to find in myself.

When I was a little girl, I didn't fully appreciate the traditional styles of dance I was learning. As I got older, I grew more and more grateful to Usha Aunty for teaching me about Indian culture through those dances. I learned much more than just the movements. I learned about Indian women and my culture. These dances were a part of the daily rituals of people in India. Many styles of Indian folk dance were originated by women who would sing in rhythm to avoid the monotony of their everyday chores. These dances evolved as entertainment from fetching water from wells (Ghada dance), leveling the ground during construction (Tippani dance), or cleaning grains from the husks after a good harvest (Supada dance). In America, all of the elegant and esteemed dancers I saw then were white. But from Usha Aunty I was introduced to the hardworking and equally beautiful women of India and their way of life. It made me feel more connected to my mother and to my grandmothers in India, whom I only saw once every few years. Learning about my ancestors made me appreciate and feel more deeply connected to my family heritage.

Growing up, I heard America being called "a melting pot," and much of my life was spent trying to assimilate into this stew, similar to many first- and second-generation immigrants. But what I learned from Usha Aunty was that instead of blending in, I had a richness of flavor to add.

Later, when I was in college, I had an opportunity to study dance academically. While watching various performances, I was deeply impacted by the sorrowful, soulful, and hopeful *Revelations*, choreographed by Alvin Ailey. Inspired by African American history and culture, this dance embodied both the horrors of slavery and the joys of faith and community. Through these experiences, I discovered that dance can be a meaningful way to express more than movement. It is an incredibly trans-formative and transcendental way to convey a deep message. I witnessed how culture can be represented onstage and can break through barriers. I saw my potential in the world—my identity as a dancer and an Indian woman. All of this knowledge helped me become comfortable in my own skin and body.

Sometimes we avoid parts of our identities when we don't know much about them. These identities can feel "foreign" even to ourselves, and we have to make a conscious effort to embrace them. For instance, after creating ClassPass, I was often referred to as a tech entrepreneur, but I shied away from that identity because my background was more in business than engineering. But over time, as we continued designing and refining ClassPass, I grew more comfortable with this descriptor and even proud of it. It isn't the only thing I am, but it is a part of who I am, and I have learned to embrace it.

EMBRACE YOUR IDENTITY AND LET IT SHINE

Are there parts of your identity that you shy away from? Or aspects of your life or history that you downplay or hide from others because you don't want to appear different? Becoming comfortable with ourselves, and becoming comfortable with ourselves in front of others, are two different things, and both can be lifelong challenges.

Eventually, we often learn that it's not easy to bring our whole self into every room. Inevitably, some aspects of our identity will not be well received by everyone. This is one reason we often act like "different people" in different contexts. However, while standing out can be a stressful experience, it can also help us achieve our goals.

Even the most seemingly superficial differences can make us feel less than or like we don't belong. But there are always ways to flip this around and use those differences to stand out in a powerfully positive way.

When I was in college, I interviewed for my very first consultant internship. We were tasked with presenting and leading a conversation on a certain topic. There were six of us around the table, and we each took turns. As I watched one candidate stand up and walk to the front of the table, I started to sweat. I was up next. I knew the group assumed that when it was my turn, I would stand up and give my presentation just like her. I didn't want to do that.

At four-foot-eleven, I'd spent my whole life feeling incredibly uncomfortable speaking in front of a group. I was fine while sitting around a table, since then everyone was eye-to-eye. But as soon as I stood up, I knew the first thing everyone would notice would be my height. Even worse, I'd be distracted worrying about what everyone was thinking, and I didn't want to let something as unimportant as my height keep me from getting this job.

So I came up with a plan. I didn't know if it was the right thing to do, but it was right for me. Instead of getting up and presenting at the head of the table, I stayed in my seat and led the conversation from there. Everyone was immediately surprised, as no one else had done that. But I felt so much more confident being able to look everyone in the eye, and the discussion flowed effortlessly. People conversed easily in my section because I was sitting with them versus speaking at them. I have no doubt that because of their comfort—and mine—it was a much more productive, interactive conversation than if I had been standing before the group. My unconventional move paid off, and I got the job. And the reason I did wasn't just because no one had ever done that before, but because it allowed me to be my most confident self.

Ultimately, I believe my early years struggling to feel like my whole self have formed the backbone of any success I've achieved. That experience taught me how to get comfortable being different in every room. And it motivated me to create environments in which I felt comfortable. One of my personal goals when founding ClassPass was to create a professional environment that fit me. I found it validating to create a culture where wearing leggings and going to class midday was normal (without anyone judging you!); where going from creating marketing materials to crunching numbers in Excel was a part of my daily routine; where being a woman, a dancer, and a passionate human being were powerful assets. It helped that when I started ClassPass, I had six years of professional experience and the confidence that had come from starting Sa Dance Company. I was able to walk into any room knowing how I wanted to present myself and my company. If people didn't believe in me, I knew I would find someone else who would. After splitting my identity for so long, I never wanted to be boxed in again. I'm a dancer *and* I'm a businessperson. I'm short *and* I'm powerful. I'm Indian *and* I'm American, and so on.

Reaching this place of acceptance was the result of struggling for years to be many things at once. We all contain multitudes. We are all unique. And struggling to come to terms with our identity is normal.

We are at our finest when we wear our
differences with pride.

ALTER YOUR ENVIRONMENTS

Take a moment to reflect on the circumstances in your life when you feel like you can be your fullest, most authentic self. Depending on the environment, you may feel that one strand of your identity shines the brightest or that you have to hide some aspect of yourself. When one of my friends is considering a career change, the first thing I ask is whether they are living with a dual identity—acting as one person at work and another person the rest of the time. To some extent, it's both common and to be expected that we adjust our behavior depending on the context, and different sides of our personalities naturally come out around different people. But this is distinct from adopting wholly different personas.

To embrace your full identity, investigate which aspects of yourself you keep hidden and why. Seek to understand the people and environments that prompt you to adjust yourself. Write down your answers to the following questions:

1   Which people and groups do you feel the most comfortable around?

2   Are there parts of yourself that you only reveal to certain people?

3   What makes you uncomfortable sharing those parts with the other people in your life?

Understanding how you feel around other people is the first step in embracing your authentic self. Ultimately, the goal is to spend most of your time in environments where you feel most comfortable. If that's a struggle, think about ways to show more of yourself in current life situations.

> Remember, see the things that make you different as strengths, not weaknesses. As you become more comfortable with your full, authentic self, this will also help others feel more comfortable with the totality of who you are.

SHARE THE TOTALITY OF YOU

In the spring of 2007, while working as a consultant at Bain, I had an upcoming dance showcase. I wanted to invite a few of my coworkers to come see it, but I didn't want to offend the rest of my colleagues by not inviting them, so I wrestled with who to send the invitation to. I was scared that some coworkers might not take me seriously if they saw my passion for dance. Maybe I was still haunted by the third-grade talent show, but I was keenly aware that in the almost three years I'd been working there none of my peers had invited the staff to anything like this showcase. We all worked eighty-hour weeks in addition to trips, retreats, team-building, and social events, leaving most people no time to pursue hobbies or passions on the side. No one really revealed their outside-of-work selves. I didn't even know if some people even had an outside-of-work identity!

My anxiety over what my colleagues would think of me reflected the idea, which is common in business, that if we have outside interests, then we are somehow less effective at our jobs. However, I knew for myself that dance gave me the creative energy to do better work, and I wanted some of my peers to see me in my element. I didn't want to feel guilty over the activity I loved the most, and I certainly wasn't going to give it up. This feeling is what ultimately made me hit *send* on that email and invite the entire two-hundred-person New York City staff to the showcase.

If you could have your coworkers see you do
one thing outside of work, what would it be?
Being in your element can reveal so much about
who you are and what you love.

I was touched by how many of my colleagues came, and to my surprise, something shifted at work after that performance. My peers and even my bosses recognized my talents and passion for dance, and afterward, they were more understanding when I had to skip late-night meetings or company dinners to go to rehearsal. One of the partners at the firm even asked me to teach him and his fiancée a dance for their upcoming wedding. It was a complete role reversal to go to his house on the weekends and be the one in charge. It gave me more confidence when we were in work meetings together. It gave me more confidence in dance, too. I believe it's what made me feel ready to start Sa.

When we compartmentalize our identity, we aren't bringing our fullest self to what we do. By limiting our identity, we limit what we're capable of. During each stage of my career, I became more comfortable being my full, authentic self, and this continued when I built ClassPass, which benefited from my many facets coming together. The very concept of ClassPass emerged from my deepening sense of self, and my ability to embrace both my creative and business sides. My passion for dance had kept me closely connected to a class environment, so I knew the challenges people faced when searching for and booking classes. Meanwhile, as a woman in tech, I had a fresh perspective that gave me direct insight into our target customers, who were mostly women. I was able to speak to their challenges and desires because I was part of that community.

As time went on, instead of hiding who I was or running away from certain aspects of myself, I felt that someone could never truly know me until they saw me dance, the magnetic force that led me everywhere in life.

Four years after starting ClassPass, I was invited to be the keynote speaker at the Salesforce Dreamforce event in San Francisco. This conference is one of the biggest tech conferences of the year and attracts more than 170,000 attendees. ClassPass was an early user of one of Salesforce's new products, and they wanted to showcase how we used their service and how they were helping new entrepreneurs. The conference coordinators said they welcomed any kind of creative presentation that would catch people's attention, and I knew instantly what I wanted to do.

With dancers from the Sa Dance Company, I choreographed a piece that would be performed before my speech. This was my way of demonstrating how my love for Indian dance had inspired me to start ClassPass, and it would highlight the company's mission of creating that spark for other people. My keynote address would present my complete identity on that stage, both Indian dancer and tech entrepreneur.

Thankfully, the performance went as planned, and I was delighted that the audience was engaged in the colorful cultural piece. As soon as it was over, I took five minutes to change into a more comfortable outfit and come back out onstage to give my keynote address. Unlike when I was a high school cheerleader and felt the need to scrub off all traces of my other identity, this time I came out still wearing my jewelry, with my bangles jingling. This signaled to myself and others that I was no longer hiding or compartmentalizing my identities. My whole self got me to that stage—literally and figuratively—and so I presented my whole self.

As my profile as a female entrepreneur grew and the importance of women in such roles commanded more attention, something unexpected happened. I was asked by iconic brands like Nike, Tumi, and Delta to be featured in their ad campaigns. While this was a fun change of pace for a tech-company founder who was used to being in meetings all day, mostly I appreciated becoming, I hope, an inspiration for little girls like me. Growing up, I never saw anyone who looked like me in TV ads or magazines, and I never imagined that someone like me could ever be in those ads. Sometimes, we don't see ourselves, or our particular identities, reflected in the world, but that doesn't mean we don't belong. That doesn't mean we have to hide our differences. We should embrace our full selves. After all, our differences might be what get us noticed and become the fuel for our success. No one else in the world has the exact same combination of traits and experiences as you—that's invaluable. Nothing has made me happier than showing the world that leaders can come in all genders, ethnicities, and, in my case, a four-foot-eleven size!

My differences make me exceptional.

3

EXPECTATIONS

Whose life are you living?

AS I WAS GROWING UP, my parents drilled into me that getting a good education was the most important thing in the world. They told me that I had to get good grades and that even an A-minus wasn't acceptable, and this set the bar for my performance. After college, they encouraged me to be ambitious, get a prestigious job, and give my career my all. I deeply respected my parents and wanted to prove that their sacrifices for me were worthwhile, so I climbed the traditional ladder of success rung by rung. This story is no doubt familiar to anyone from an Indian family, and I know it occurs in many families and cultures.

That said, as soon as I landed a coveted job, my mother almost immediately shifted her message and started pressuring me to get married! While I realized that this reflected my mom's upbringing, this 180-degree turnaround felt like a bait-and-switch. I felt very confused about what success was supposed to look like for me.

Every day I called my mom on my way to work. She was and is a very strong presence in my life, and she was always encouraging me and pushing me to excel. I usually loved our chats in the morning, but not so much once marriage took center stage. Trying to sound casual, she would always ask who I was (or, more accurately, wasn't) dating: "So, Payal, tell me, have you met anyone new?" As I wove through the crowds crossing the streets in Midtown Manhattan, I tried to stop myself from rolling my eyes.

"No, I'm not dating anyone," I usually responded.

"You should try to find more time to date," she inevitably replied.

She didn't mean to make me feel bad, but these conversations sent me spiraling. Dating in New York City was hard, and somehow I always picked the wrong people. My friends were dating or in serious relationships, and I felt incomplete being single, not to mention lonely.

My mom's voice in my ear added extra pressure. My mother had always been very clear that she worked so hard at her multiple jobs to save money for two things: her daughters' educations and her daughters' weddings. By the time I graduated from MIT and started working, my sister had a college degree and a husband. My mother had checked off three out of four of the goals on her list, and her constant refrain to me became "I'll retire on the day you get married." In other words, my being single was holding up her retirement!

The longer this went on, without me fulfilling her dream, the more my daily phone calls with my mom became a source of stress and worry. Worse, every time I met someone new or went out on a date, all I thought about was how I would summarize the date for my mom. I found myself asking my date the same questions I knew my mother would ask me instead of letting the conversation flow naturally. I focused more on whether I thought my mom would like a guy than if I was interested in him myself.

Everybody receives messages from family, friends, teachers, bosses, communities, and even social media about the way life should be, and this influences our expectations for our lives. Sometimes the messages are directed specifically at us, and sometimes they are directed at people in general, and they can pertain to any aspect of life: how we should act and dress and behave, what careers we should pursue, where to live, and whether or not to get married—and to whom. Whether we're aware of it or not, this messaging seeps into our minds from a very young age, setting our expectations for what is possible— and these messages can both unleash and limit our potential.

My mother's focus on my dating life stemmed from a place of love and concern, but she was inadvertently putting the idea in my head that I was incomplete and failing to move forward in life if I wasn't on the path to getting married. This magnified the emptiness and insecurities that I already felt. There were important things I wanted to accomplish in life, and I didn't want to feel that I had to find Mr. Right at the expense of my career or dreams, or worse that I needed a guy to take care of me. I didn't want to settle for the wrong person, either. It took me a long time to realize that what I did with my life was my deci- sion—this being one of the most important I would ever make.

It's not uncommon to struggle to balance what we really want with the expectations of others, but we won't ever feel successful if we're chasing someone else's definition of success. Sometimes getting clear about what we want can be challenging, but through practice we can clarify success on our own terms— and only then can we start reaching for it.

WHOSE LIFE ARE YOU LIVING?

What expectations do you have for your life, and where do those expectations come from? Have you been going along with someone else's ideas of who you should be and what you should do? Even if you don't always follow it, can you distinguish your own voice from that of others?

Take a moment to reflect on the expectations and influences that have shaped your life so far. Answer these questions to explore what has impacted your decisions and priorities:

1 Write down a few important decisions you've recently made in your life. This can be your education, a hobby, where to live, what job to take, and/or what relationships to pursue.

2 To what extent were you thinking about other people when you made these decisions? Who were you thinking of in each situation?

3 Imagine making these same decisions without considering the opinions of others. What if you only listened to yourself? Would the outcome have been any different, and in what ways?

Of course, sometimes we seek the guidance and advice of others, but this is different from feeling obligated to do what others think is right. After answering these questions, reflect on how successful you are at setting your own expectations for your life. Then, keep tuning in to your own voice so it can be your guide.

SET BOUNDARIES

In the early days of ClassPass, I worked around the clock, as any start-up company requires. While this left even less time for me to think about dating, it was still on the top of my mom's mind. The daily phone calls didn't change, but I had more important things to think about. I was following my calling and marching to work fueled with the passion to make a difference in the world. Starting the day by talking to my mom about my lackluster love life put me off my game—and it's not like these calls were getting me any closer to her dream of me getting married.

Furthermore, I deeply wanted to please her and make her proud. But I needed to figure out what I wanted without her perspective taking over my mind. Plus, I had a company to build! It wasn't helpful to start a day of grinding and problem solving by hearing my mother ask, "Why aren't you dating?" It made me feel bad to always be coming up short in this department.

I had to find a way to turn down the volume of my mother's voice. I did this by taking control of our morning conversations. I set up a boundary around my dating life. Every time she brought it up, I'd simply say, "Mom, I have to go. I have a meeting. I love you." With that, I would end the conversation. It helped me to feel I had some control over the situation. I didn't have to talk to her about my dating life, and I didn't have to let her worries overtake my mind.

When I turned thirty, my mom finally realized that I wasn't going to get married on her timeline, and she decided to retire anyway. She and my dad went to India for four months, which made it difficult for us to talk as often due to the time difference. I used this time to free myself of my mother's expectations and to try to better understand the kind of partner I actually wanted.

This freedom and open-mindedness suffused other parts of my life and made me feel much more confident as a woman and as a leader. It's no coincidence that ClassPass took many steps forward during this time. This showed me how important it is to always listen to your own voice.

When my parents came back from India, I told my mom that I didn't want to talk to her about dating and marriage anymore. I told her that the discussions wouldn't change anything, and the topic was only making us both upset. She agreed to abide by my request, but she still brought up dating every once in a while. When she did, I continued to take control of the conversation and tell her that I had to go. This allowed me to enjoy talking to my mom while avoiding being triggered. I trusted myself to maintain that boundary and not feel bad about it, which enabled me to call her with confidence and comfort.

Eventually, I met my husband and partner in life, Nick, and of course, this made my mother very happy. However, I look back on my twenties with one major regret. I had spent too much time wishing I wasn't single versus enjoying the journey. This pressure came from society's expectations as well as my mother's, and it got in the way of me being present and appreciating some of the good times. There were times when the company hit incredible milestones, and I came home at night feeling alone or believing that I was still not enough because I wasn't married. I wish I had not taken other people's expectations to heart.

The lesson of this experience is that it's essential to set boundaries with people whose voices overpower our own. This means setting and enforcing limits, whether that's avoiding certain topics or even avoiding certain people. It might mean (politely) ending the conversation with a friend or relative who wants to tell us how to live or turning off the phone and exiting social media to avoid fostering self-doubt.

Consider whether there are any specific relationships in your life that would benefit from some boundaries. Are there friends who make you feel bad about yourself or colleagues who are always bringing you down? If someone's voice is overpowering yours, it's important to turn down their volume so you can hear your own thoughts. This doesn't mean ignoring or tuning out everyone who challenges or disagrees with us. But if you notice a pattern in which the feedback of certain friends, colleagues, or family members leads you to question yourself and your decisions, it's time to take control.

Most of the time, this simply means setting a boundary and maintaining it. Get clear about what boundary you want to establish and come up with a plan to enforce it. If there are topics you want to avoid, either tell the other person that you don't want to discuss those topics or find a way to end the conversation when these subjects come up. How you set a boundary and what kind often depends on the specific relationship. Occasionally, however, you might need to take a temporary break from a person (or in extreme cases, end a negative relationship).

The goal of boundaries is to avoid one or both people becoming triggered in ways that damage the relationship (and adversely affect you). I define a triggering topic as one that derails us from the things we want to be thinking about. This is similar to maintaining a healthy diet by eliminating certain foods. If we want to maintain a healthy mindset, we can eliminate talking about certain topics (or with certain people about those topics). We don't have to consume anyone else's thoughts about how we should live. We can listen and take advice when it's helpful, while always making up our own minds about the best path for ourselves.

> *We can't control other people, but we*
> *can set boundaries and limits. We don't*
> *have to talk about anything we don't*
> *want to. Everything we allow into our*
> *mind is food for thought.*

REFRAME YOUR RELATIONSHIP WITH EXPECTATIONS

In order to break free of the confines of expectations, it's important to get to the root of them. Though I didn't see it at the time, I now understand that my mom's expectations weren't about me, but about her. It was the contract she had with Indian society to see her daughters marry. She was reacting to ideas that were centuries old and embedded deeply within her. What she really wanted was for me to be surrounded by love and security, which was something that I wanted for myself, too. After raising money from various investors for my company, I heard a lot from those investors about their opinions and expectations. In time, I learned that the pressure I felt from them was sometimes coming from other partners at their firm or the people who invested in their funds. Their expectations weren't always about me as a founder or a reflection of my work.

This is true for many people. They react to others based on their own experiences. Every person must deal with the expectations that have been placed on them and which they then often place on others. When we look at it this way, it allows us to have more understanding and empathy, rather than always taking expectations and criticisms personally. Thinking about it in this vein has helped me to have better relationships with my family, with bosses, with investors—and it has enabled me to clarify my own expectations for myself and others.

It has also enabled me to see the positive side of expectations. While giving too much weight to external voices can adversely affect us, other voices can also provide inspiration. Usha Aunty has put expectations on me my whole life, but I don't experience this as negative or limiting. When I was a child, what she expected was not that I follow the path she or someone else laid out for me. She simply demanded that I give my best at all times, both inside and outside of dance class. And more, she pushed me beyond what I thought I could do—something she still does! When Kamala Harris became the vice president of the United States, Usha Aunty sent me a text: "Payal, something to think about? . . . I am serious, please start now."

By reframing our relationship with expectations, we can discover guides who can inspire a new definition of success. How do we know if an expectation is good or bad? How do we distinguish between motivation and obligation? The best way to decipher this is to think about what would happen if we didn't do something. Would the consequences be more disappointing to ourselves or someone else? If it's us, we can use that expectation as a motivator to push ourselves further. If it's someone else, then we might recognize it as an obligation. In that case, we might still do what someone wanted, or we might consider the worst thing that might happen if we didn't fulfill that expectation. In a healthy relationship, if the worst outcome is the other person's disappointment, most people and relationships would recover.

When I worked at Bain, I was also surrounded by a network of dancers who were on an alternate, more creative path than mine. They revealed another option that I never knew existed. These women weren't that different from me. Many came from families that were similar to mine. Yet unlike me, they were chasing creative careers, and this painted a picture of possibilities for me that I'd never dreamed of before.

In this group was a professional dancer, an artist, and an editor. They were all older, and I looked up to them as people who were living their passions. As we spent more and more time together, dancing in one of our living rooms or obsessing over a certain piece of music after rehearsal, they amplified my creative side and inspired me to think differently and bigger about my life. While we are all individuals, we are also products of our environment, and we are greatly influenced by the people who are in it. As the adage goes, we are the average of the five people we spend the most time with.

Sometimes, the people who shape us the most aren't even the people in our lives. From an early age I was in awe of Bollywood actresses, and later I was obsessed with Beyoncé and J.Lo. I admired them all as women and creatives. My dream wasn't to be onstage like them (well, maybe a little), but I loved how they owned their lives—their careers, personalities, and beings. I looked up to these women because I believed they were doing what they loved. I didn't know them, but they embodied the freedom to live life on your own terms.

Take a moment to consider who has shaped your ideas, aspirations, and worldview. Who do you follow, read, and watch?

Who do you talk to and share ideas with? Are they serving you well? Make an effort to follow and learn from role models you admire and who inspire you. The point is not to be like someone else but to use their light to help us find our own. We know that we've found the right people because they will help us hear our own voice instead of drowning it out with their own opinions or negative thoughts. As a company founder, I have advisors to help me make business decisions. I've found that the most effective advisors ask questions about the situation. Instead of telling me what to do, they ask, "What do you think you should do?"

With someone who understands us and who makes us feel completely comfortable, we are better able to hear ourselves clearly and express what we want, our truth. Do you have people in your life like this, those who help amplify your own voice? Foster those connections.

FALSE SIGNALS OF SUCCESS

When I first became an entrepreneur and started ClassPass, I followed in the footsteps of other folks I knew who had started companies. I built an expert team, reached out to investors, applied to incubators—and did everything that anyone who knew anything about start-ups told me to do. Starting a company was new to me, and I didn't really know how to measure success, so I used other people's benchmarks. For instance, before launch, other founders I knew and articles I read emphasized the importance of having an amazing home page design, so my team and I spent hours trying to be the gold standard. We also made sure that we were collecting email addresses from every person we could think of to continue to grow our email list—which checked another box that was deemed important for every start-up. We garnered press and even ended up on the cover of *Inc.* magazine before launching.

By every standard I knew, we were doing the right things. But despite meeting all these expectations, we soon learned they were giving us a false sense of success. We had built a beautiful product, the colors on the home page were just right, and we launched to some fanfare . . . and then we didn't see any bookings come through that day, that evening, the next day, and so on. That's because we forgot to focus on the only expectation that mattered—getting people to class!

To succeed, we had to jettison the expectations of Silicon Valley. Social media, brand partnerships, and press hits were not our leading indicators of success. These false signals of success shielded us from seeing the real problems that were right in front of us. We hadn't fully understood the challenges our customers were facing in getting to class. No matter how many articles were written about our company or how much money we raised, if people weren't signing up for classes, then we weren't making progress toward our mission, and we certainly did not have a business that would support our future. We needed to focus on the reason the company was created in the first place. Reservations were the most important metric.

So I changed my approach and focused all our energy on solving that problem and delivering what we promised to our customers. This shift united and energized the company. It also showed me something important: You can transform expectations into a mission that becomes a driving force.

This lesson translates into our personal lives as well. There is no blueprint for your journey. Like an entrepreneur, you set the expectations for your "company," and you decide how to spend your resources and time to achieve your goals, your purpose. As a society, we tend to conflate the idea of success with achievement. When someone accomplishes a specific goal or reaches a new milestone in their life or career, we view that as success. You get a raise: success. A new job: success. Launch a new company: success. Marriage: success. Kids: success. A new house: success. And those things might be experienced as success, but they are not the end of the journey. They are all moments in time. They are all the beginnings of the rest of the journey.

Sometimes, these successes can lead to failure or take us in a wrong direction. Look back and consider: Have you ever been blinded by false expectations or false signs of success? To some extent, this happens to everyone. We are conditioned by society to chase certain signs of success, or to measure success in certain ways. Some signs are highly prized simply because they're measurable and can be counted, like social media followers, income, meetings you attend, and pounds on a scale. It's also easy to compare job titles, cars, and homes.

These false signals of success are seductive, and we can end up chasing what's easy to see—fame, money, power, and so on—instead of what's harder to quantify: love, passion, and purpose. Likewise, if we let the perceptions of others drive our lives, we can get pushed further and further away from our calling, so that finding happiness or satisfaction becomes nearly impossible.

The point isn't that material success is bad, nor is there anything wrong with wanting more money, a nicer house, or a better job. The point is to know ourselves and to define for ourselves what really matters to us, our life purpose. Then, to make sure that what we're doing supports that passion and purpose, rather than fulfilling what someone else defines as success. When we set our own expectations and goals, and make decisions rooted in our own sense of purpose, then it's easier to identify the false signals of success and avoid the wrong turns that lead to failure in what matters most to us. Take a moment and ask yourself: *What truly motivates you? What drives you and inspires love, passion, and purpose? What is your definition of success?*

WHAT IS FUELING YOUR ACTIONS?

SELF-CHECK POINT

Whether our actions are fulfilling or not often depends on our intentions. This exercise is a way to explore your intentions and consider if your expectations are contributing to your purpose or pulling you in a wrong direction.

Write down three to five recent actions you took, both big and small. Next to each one, write down your intentions, expectations, or motivations behind the action. Often, we have more than one. Write down as many as you like, but also identify which reason was the most important. Here are some examples to get you started.

Took a position at work for the title	**POWER**
Went to an event primarily to post on social media	**FAME**
Mentored someone at work because I saw their potential	**PURPOSE**
Tried a new painting class	**PASSION**

Review the list and consider whether you see any patterns. Chances are that you have more positive emotions associated with the choices that were fueled by love, passion, and purpose than power, fame, and greed. The ultimate goal is to have all of your decisions motivated by love, passion, and purpose so that you can lead a happier, more satisfying life.

Ultimately, we can't control how our choices turn out, but we can always control what we do and for what reason. Use this exercise as a way to increase your awareness of what your intentions and expectations are, and use that awareness to make sure your actions align with your calling and don't simply become a false signal of success.

INVITE SUPPORT ON YOUR JOURNEY

Even as we identify our life purpose, and even as we align our actions with our intentions, we still can't make the journey alone. This is something I learned after I left Bain and gained the strength to truly go after what I wanted: We have to get others on board. We need a support network. This is another reason we need to be our authentic self at all times and not compartmentalize our identity based on what we think others will think of us. When we share our full selves and our life purpose with everyone we meet, this is one way we invite them to help us and join us on our journey. Not everyone will, of course, and gathering support isn't always easy. But when we actively invite support, we might be surprised by who shows up.

This is what happened with my parents. After I left Bain to work at Warner, my dad was still hoping I'd eventually go to business school. He assumed I had made this career change so that I'd have more time to study for the GMAT, and I did not have the heart to correct him. A few days before our first Sa Dance Company studio showcase, he called and said, "I'm worried that you're not spending enough time studying. Tell me again, what is the date of the test?"

I didn't know what to say. I hadn't signed up to take the GMAT, and I had no intention of doing so. But I just couldn't bear disappointing my dad. I worried that if I told my parents I didn't want to go to business school, it would be disrespectful of the sacrifices they'd made in order to give me the chance to go to business school in the first place. To my parents, dance or anything creative didn't provide a secure career. I knew that I couldn't live out the rest of *my* life chasing *their* definition of success, but I still felt too guilty to be honest.

"Dad, I need to focus on our studio showcase right now," I said. "The GMATs will still be there after it's over."

"But you need to study! You can't keep dancing so much if it's keeping you from getting an education." My dad didn't usually voice strong opinions, and for the first time in my life, I could hear that I was letting him down. I held back tears until we hung up the phone, then I let them out.

Nevertheless, as much as my parents wanted me to focus on my education, they also supported my efforts with Sa. At the studio showcase, they sat in the first row, and the small room was packed with 150 people, though the space was only meant to hold half that number. My promotional efforts included a Facebook event post and invitations sent to everyone I knew, but word had spread throughout the South Asian community. Shocked by the standing-room-only crowd, I thought to myself, *People really showed up.*

The performance itself was greeted with a standing ovation, and I was completely elated by Sa's success. The next day, I got an even bigger surprise. My dad called, and I prepared myself for another argument. Instead, he said, "There are some good arts programs at Columbia. Do you want me to look into MFA programs for you?"

This time I fought back happy tears, realizing that my dad saw and respected the hard work I had put into creating something meaningful through dance. Seeing how our community had responded proved to him that I was making progress toward something positive, even if it wasn't exactly what he was familiar with or expected. I knew this change of heart wasn't easy for him, and in a way, he hadn't changed. His first focus was education, which for him was still the most important thing.

Of course, not everyone in our lives will understand or support what we choose to do or consider important. This is one reason it can be tempting to compartmentalize our lives; it's a way to avoid conflict, particularly with people we love. But if we only tell those people about the pieces of our life that we think they'll understand, we might also be robbing them of an opportunity to change their minds. Others might surprise themselves and us by accepting our invitation to help us on our journey.

After the studio showcase, I made sure to keep my parents updated with every tiny bit of good news. I shared every positive article and email about Sa so my parents could see firsthand that I was making an impact and contributing something meaningful to the world, particularly for the Indian community. Every time we were asked to perform or received a compliment, I forwarded it to them. I wanted them to feel that this success was theirs as much as mine. I continued to do this as I embarked on becoming an entrepreneur, a career path that was unknown and must have been terrifying to my parents, who grew up in such a different generation. Not only did I invite others to help me strategize and formulate the concept of ClassPass, I kept my parents involved, sharing all the positive feedback I received. When someone offered to help or to invest in the company, I called and told them. Over time, they began to trust that I could do anything I put my mind to.

One Thanksgiving, while I was still researching the concept of ClassPass and working at Warner, I was at my parents' house and feeling down about having to go back to work on Monday.

"What's wrong, Payal?" my mom asked as I sat at the kitchen table. She knew me so well and could tell that something was bothering me.

I sighed, and decided to be honest. "Mom, I'm dreading going back to work tomorrow," I told her. "It's not what I want to be doing."

I expected my mom to say something about appreciating that I had a well-paying job or applying to grad school. Instead, she said, "Payal, I believe whatever you do in life, you're going to do it well. So if you feel really strongly, then you should quit."

I couldn't believe it. My prudent Indian mother, who'd always told me to get the best job and have security above all else, was suggesting that I quit with no established backup plan! I realized in that moment that I had earned the trust of both my parents. This meant everything to me, and having their support helped me take the biggest leap of my career.

The most important voice to listen to is my own.

Anjula that I was considering the opportunity. "What do you think?" I asked.

Anjula didn't hesitate. "Payal, if you are not willing to bet on yourself and focus on building your own company, then why would anyone else?"

I felt embarrassed. After pitching my start-up idea, one I wholeheartedly believed in, I undermined it by revealing I had a plan B. Why would I do that? Why was I displaying my doubt? In fact, why was I so filled with doubt in the first place?

Looking back, I realize that I'd always had a backup plan, in part because I'd absorbed my parents' aversion to risk. It gave me comfort, like a security blanket. Even though I wanted to be an entrepreneur, I believed that the responsible thing to do was to have another job in the wings in case my ClassPass idea didn't work out. Having a backup plan didn't seem like a negative thing. It seemed strategic and prudent.

In some cases, that can be true. But after our meeting, Anjula's words kept replaying in my head, and they made me realize that having a contingency plan was also my way of shielding myself from failure. I was afraid of failing. I was afraid of betting everything on myself and not having it work out. If it didn't, what would that say about me, and what would my parents think? Yet I knew Anjula was right: If I wanted to succeed, if I wanted others to believe in me, I had to be 100 percent committed and not let any doubt stand in my way. That night, I stayed up working on a business plan that answered all the questions she had raised about the business, and I sent it to her at 3 a.m. knowing this was the only way to move forward. After that moment, I never looked back. I didn't need a plan B.

This moment finally gave me the courage to quit my job. I had a business plan, my parents' blessing, and the confidence to pursue my calling. The day I quit, I was filled with all kinds of emotions, from excitement to fear. Then I got a message from the vice chairman of Warner asking me to come to his office. He wanted to hear about what I was doing next. During my three years at Warner, I had hardly interacted with him, so I was surprised that he wanted to talk to me now that I was leaving. Sitting in the leather chair in his corner office, he asked about my plans.

When I was finished, he said, "I'd like to invest." He also made another compelling offer. "I'm going to introduce you to David Tisch."

I couldn't believe it! On the day I quit—one of the most frightening career decisions in my life—I ended up with a check for ten thousand dollars and a connection to David Tisch, who was heading up Techstars, one of the hottest tech incubators in NYC. I couldn't believe how people were responding to my departure and my plans. Many of my colleagues offered to help in any way they could. No one thought this was a bad idea. On the contrary, many people actually had looks of admiration on their faces, almost as if they wished they could leave and work on something that they loved. For years, I'd been measuring myself against the success of these people and feeling that I was constantly coming up short. But as soon as I overcame doubt and committed fully to what I believed in, others viewed me differently. I finally understood what leadership expert Robin Sharma meant when he said, "On the other side of your greatest fears lives your greatest life."

Are you living your plan A or plan B?

If you're living your plan B, what's

holding you back from your plan A?

FAILURE IS A DATA POINT, NOT AN END POINT

A year and a half after visiting my friend Parul in San Francisco for her birthday party—where I challenged myself to come up with an entrepreneurial idea—I headed back seeking to raise money for that very idea. I was confident; up to then, everything was going well. To help me build ClassPass, I had teamed up with my friend Sanjiv Sanghavi, whom I'd known since I was five years old. With my former boss's connection, we had a foot in the door at Techstars and were one of only fourteen companies selected to participate out of fifteen hundred applicants. Thanks to this program, we had the opportunity to network with well-known entrepreneurs, raise money from angel investors, receive media coverage, and gather ten thousand email addresses to add to our mailing list. When I added together all the milestones we'd reached, it felt like we had already succeeded. But as you know, those milestones were only false signals of success.

In San Francisco, we had three whirlwind days of back-to-back meetings with big-name venture capitalist (VC) firms. All seemed to go smoothly, and we were told that if a firm was going to make an offer, we would hear from them right away. So, after each meeting, we eagerly waited for an email or a call. Each night, we stayed up waiting, but no email or phone call ever came. None of the firms we met with wanted to give us money. A pit started forming in my stomach.

To make matters worse, the news from the rest of the team in New York was dire: No one was signing up for classes on our newly launched website. Looking at our analytics, we could see that people were visiting the site and browsing, but they weren't following through on booking a class.

I flew home feeling frustrated, disappointed, and even a bit scared. We had completed a prestigious accelerator program, launched the website, and met with top-notch VC firms, and yet no one was investing and no customers were booking. My previous doubts crept back. *Could I pull this off? What would happen if this didn't work? What about all the people—my existing investors and my team—who were depending on me? What was I going to do?*

I felt the pressure building and I started to question everything. Thankfully, we still had some money from our early angel investors, which would give us time to identify and fix the problem. Back in New York, we regrouped and decided to retool the site so it would encourage visitors to book classes. We assumed the issue was with the site layout and the user interface.

In what I'll forever remember as "the summer of buttons," we spent July and August of 2012 tweaking the site, but none of the superficial changes made a difference. By September, our customers had only booked a total of a hundred classes through the site. Our models had predicted that people would have booked at least ten thousand classes by that time.

In desperation, we sent a blast to our ten thousand email subscribers offering them a free class if they booked it with us. That evening, I sat in our office and checked to see how many customers had used the promotion. Not a single person had taken us up on the offer. After over a year and a half, I was exhausted—and starting to feel defeated. Normally, whenever I put the work in, I got results, but that wasn't happening this time.

This became my lowest moment. I felt like a failure. I'd wake up in the middle of the night replaying the doubts my investors had expressed: "Do people really need this product?" "This would work better to book personal training sessions." "There are a lot of companies tackling this space, but we're not yet sure there is a big enough market." I thought about giving up, returning the money I'd taken from our initial investors, and going back to something more comfortable.

One day, I phoned one of my advisors and confessed I was tempted to give up. He didn't hold back. "Payal, this is on you," he told me. "You still have cash in the bank and a problem to solve in the world, and your current product isn't solving it. So what are you going to do? You have to move forward."

He was right. I realized that I had to clear my mind of all the doubts and fears and instead focus on the original problem I wanted to solve. I realized I was still 100 percent committed to our mission, and that commitment overrode everything else, even the horrible feeling of failure. This is the reason it's so important to have a mission we are deeply passionate about. If I had cared even 1 percent less, I wouldn't have had the resilience to keep fighting.

Starting over was intimidating, but at the same time, I needed to flip the conversation in my head. I had been telling myself that I was a failure, but in reality, I had simply gone down the wrong path.

There are many ways to solve a problem, and multiple options for how to take action. It's like trying to negotiate a maze. If you take a wrong turn and reach a dead end, does that mean you've failed? No, you only fail if you give up or stay stagnant, or if you keep trying to solve the maze by doing the same thing over and over again. No matter how many options you try or how long it takes, if you keep moving and learning from any missteps, you will find the path that leads to success.

That said, reaching a dead end can feel like failure, and fear of failure often keeps us from taking action toward our dreams. What I've learned throughout my life, but especially when launching ClassPass, is that failure is a data point, not an end point. It is an opportunity to discover which directions to avoid, just as success often tells us which directions to pursue. In this way, success and failure are deeply connected. You can't have one without the other. Both are stops on the path toward our purpose. In fact, we often learn more from failure than success, and sometimes failure teaches us the exact thing we need in order to succeed. In many ways, failure can be good and necessary. We may not celebrate it like we celebrate landing our dream job or getting married, but that doesn't mean we need to fear it, either. That fear, more than failure itself, is often what stands in our way.

WHAT'S STOPPING YOU? | SELF-CHECK POINT

Too often, when we make a misstep, we get caught up in what went wrong and how bad we feel for "failing," rather than using the experience as a learning opportunity to discover what new directions or actions we might take to solve the problem. Whenever you make a misstep or are unsure of your next move, whether not getting a job or facing a breakup, ask yourself the following questions:

1   What did I learn from this?

2   What was not working?

3   What was working?

> Right now, take a moment to think about a time when you "failed." Put aside how you felt about what happened, and answer these questions to see what you can learn. Consider what other actions you might have taken to solve the issue or find success.

DON'T BE AFRAID TO CHANGE

I learned that I couldn't let a misstep stop me, but I also learned that I needed to adapt in order to succeed. To keep moving forward, I needed to change our original strategy or approach, even if the goal was the same.

Ready to move forward, I scheduled an impromptu team meeting and announced, "We're going to launch something new!" I was nervous that the team might resist starting over, but Sanjiv and the team fed off my positive energy and expressed nothing but excitement about going in a new direction. They wanted the company to succeed as well, to make progress, improve, and pursue our mission, and as the CEO, it was my duty to lead them.

That said, I still wasn't sure what direction we should take. So our first step was to meet directly with studio owners to learn more about their businesses. We also reached out to customers to see why they weren't signing up for classes and what they really wanted out of a company like ours.

We learned from our studio partners that what they really needed was for new customers to enter their doors. We also discovered that many of them already offered a free trial class. On the customer side, we found that we needed a value proposition that was more enticing. There wasn't anything motivating them to book classes through our site, and many of them were a bit hesitant to try something new!

Right away, we saw an opportunity. What if we could bundle together trial classes at different studios so that customers could explore several new classes at a range of studios over the course of a month? When the month was up, customers would receive a discount as part of the package when returning to their favorite studios. We called the new product the Passport, and at first, we kept it super simple. We had learned that lesson after our first product flopped. We weren't going to spend time building a beautiful website around a specific product until we were certain that people wanted that product.

That Thanksgiving, I sat at my parents' kitchen table inputting schedule and class details one by one into our site manually and feeling especially grateful. Our sales had improved somewhat, and, most importantly, people were going to classes. I was happy to work through the holiday if it meant more reservations. But within a few months, we hit another road bump. Customers loved the fact that they could take a variety of classes with the Passport, but they weren't going back to the studios when the month was up to buy class packages. Our goal was for 75 percent of people who rated a studio highly to return, but only about 15 percent were actually doing so. These return customers had been our value proposition to the studio owners in exchange for giving our customers a free class. The lack of follow-through was breaking down our partnerships and our business.

Studio owners were also upset because they noticed that some customers were coming back month after month with another Passport, which wasn't how the product was supposed to work. Customers were only allowed to use the Passport for one month. If they wanted to continue going to a class after that, they were supposed to buy a package directly from the studios. When we looked at the data, we saw that customers were finding a workaround by creating multiple email addresses so they could buy more than one Passport and use the product repeatedly.

In April 2013, I sat down with the team and laid out the problems. Sanjiv and a few others were reluctant to make yet another change, especially because we were finally attracting more customers and making money! "We had a hundred thousand page views on our site this month," Sanjiv said. "Are we really going to throw that out and change the business model yet again?"

Hello, false signals of success! I nodded yes. I knew if the product wasn't working for our partners, then it wouldn't work in the long run. "There is something inherently wrong with the bundling," I told him. "We might be able to marginally improve the conversion of repeat users, but I don't think doing anything else to the product is going to improve it significantly."

I knew how hard it would be for us to pivot a second time—to convince the rest of the team to start all over again, to reframe our pitch to investors, and to convince our studio partners to buy into another new product. But the core problem that we had initially wanted to tackle remained. We didn't want to change our customers' lives for a month. We wanted to create a product that they would adopt as part of their lives long-term.

I could have seen this moment as another failure. In a way, it was another dead end. But I saw an opportunity. Our customers were clearly telling us something. They wanted to keep exploring and trying new classes month after month. Why would we stop them?

We went to our existing customers and asked them if they would use the Passport again if it meant they could go back to their favorite studios; 95 percent of them said yes. This gave us the confidence to create a subscription product that would allow customers to return to the classes they liked and continue exploring month after month.

In June, we launched a new subscription service for fitness classes, and we kept the Passport as a separate product offering for new users. Some team members were hesitant to completely change the model, and while I had a hunch this product would work, the only way to know was to put it out there. Having multiple products definitely put a stress on the team, but looking back, it was worth the extra effort. By the end of that summer, sales of the subscription had far surpassed the Passport. We were finally on the right track, but it didn't fully hit me until I was on an elevator going up to my apartment.

"It's amazing," a woman in the elevator said to her friend, "I can try all these new classes, and I'm working out so much more. I'll never go back to a regular gym." It took me a minute to process that she was talking about ClassPass! I was so shocked and overjoyed that I forgot to get off the elevator on the right floor. To me, this was a true signal that we were making progress on our mission—and that was worth all the failures.

LET YOUR FEELINGS GUIDE YOU

When I was little, my nickname was *thiku mirchu*, which means "hot pepper," because I had such strong feelings. If I got made fun of or I was feeling upset, I locked myself in my room and wouldn't come out for hours. Out of a sense of protection, my mother constantly warned me not to be so emotional, and for years, I tried to change this about myself. I believed that my strong emotions were a weakness—especially at work, where I felt pressure to lead with my head instead of my heart.

Back when we were in Techstars and gearing up for our first product launch, Sanjiv and I were in a coffee shop working on our presentation before an upcoming investor meeting. We typically spent long days in the office and would continue to work after hours. As we were absorbed by our slides, focused on finessing them to perfection, I felt someone spray something on my face. At first, I thought it must have been a friend playing a prank on me with water, but then it started to burn. I heard Sanjiv yell, "Help!" and realized this wasn't a weird joke. We were in danger. Someone had sprayed us with mace, grabbed our phones, and tried to take our laptops, but Sanjiv hit him, even though he was doubled over in blinding pain from the mace. Everything was a blur, and before I could even see again, the man had run out the door with our phones.

I have lived a relatively lucky, protected life, and I had never before been physically attacked. I had never before felt like a victim. I went into shock and dealt with it by ignoring it. Trying to forget all about what had happened and just keep going. I showed up to work the very next morning. I thought I was doing the right thing for the company by continuing to move forward.

It wasn't until months later that I realized the traumatic impact this experience had had on me. Sanjiv and I were rushing from meeting to meeting when he made a silly joke. Since childhood Sanjiv has been able to make me laugh. But this time, as I started laughing, tears began pouring out of my eyes. I hadn't let myself feel anything since the attack, and all of those suppressed emotions emerged.

Coming to terms with the attack made me see something else I had been suppressing—what wasn't working with our start-up. I was acting like what was going on with the company wasn't a problem, in the same way I had acted like being attacked wasn't a big deal. I thought I was operating with a level-headed perspective and doing what I was supposed to do as a leader.

Fast forward to the night before I called an impromptu team meeting after speaking with my advisor and accepting the failure of our first product. I sat on the couch in my apartment and cried. It felt good to release all of the fear and disappointment that had been building up over the past few months. Letting myself feel again reminded me of why I had started on this journey in the first place. It was important to connect to that why before embarking on a new path. That helped me spring into action.

When the tears finally stopped, I had total clarity about what we needed to do to learn from our mistakes and succeed. The next day when I spoke with the team about how we would keep moving forward, I let my emotions out. Matching my fervor, the team responded by putting their own hearts and souls into finding a new solution. Without those powerful emotions guiding us, we would have stayed lost.

True leaders align their heads and their hearts to find success. Living a life of passion inherently comes with highs and lows. If I was going to lead with passion, I would have to be resilient through those moments of uncertainty and missteps. As the leader of my company, I discovered my strength comes from listening to and honoring my emotions.

Some people are more comfortable expressing their feelings than others, but we should always accept and recognize our emotions. Like failure, they can at times be uncomfortable, and even shake us to our core, but they provide us with invaluable information we can learn from. We should never doubt or ignore our emotions. The more we allow ourselves to feel, the easier it becomes to manage the roller coaster of highs and lows, so we can lead with our emotions and turn them into practical actions to move forward.

All emotions are temporary. They are just the way we feel in the moment, but they are not who we are. Similarly, success and failure are both temporary. They reflect the outcomes of our efforts, but they are not who we are. That said, we have to experience whatever happens completely in order to keep moving forward. When good things happen, I like to celebrate fully right away, and then focus on the next thing. When bad things happen, I allow myself to feel whatever arises—disappointment, anger, frustration, doubt—and then move on. Today, I assess my own level of success based on how I am feeling. I set an intention to feel something and set practical goals that will help me get there. Later, during goal setting in part 3, I will help you identify the emotional state that defines success *for you*. This can help you overcome any fear of failure and keep moving forward and making progress toward your highest potential.

SIT WITH YOUR THOUGHTS

SELF-CHECK POINT

When we shy away from pain, it lingers. But if we take a moment to sit with a feeling, this allows us to bounce back and move on. This helps us get to the root of the issue, so we can understand why we are feeling a certain way and determine what to do about it.

Whenever you are feeling negative emotions, take a moment to ask yourself the following questions:

1   What is at the root of this negative feeling? Is it related to pride? Is it because I'm scared?

2   What can I do about it? What can't I do about it?

3   Have I had this feeling in the past? How did I cope?

Asking these questions might not make what's painful go away. But the first step to moving forward is acknowledging what you're feeling and figuring out how to fix whatever is upsetting you. Even if you don't discover a solution, learning how to be with and process emotions is an essential skill that helps you keep moving forward.

FOCUS ON RIGHT NOW, NOT "CHAMPAGNE PROBLEMS"

When I first started ClassPass, I dotted every *i* and crossed every *t*. That's what I thought an entrepreneur was supposed to do, and it was how I was trained as a consultant. But I soon discovered that this approach wasn't always effective or efficient. Focusing on every tiny detail made me *think* I was making progress, but in reality, I wasn't working on what was most important. My intention was to protect my company, but this sometimes kept me from building my company.

For example, one of our first orders of business was to trademark our name. I was worried about what would happen if we didn't protect it, but guess what? We changed our name three times! What a waste of money! I could have spent that money more efficiently on what we needed at the moment, rather than worrying about some potential problem down the road.

This is an example of a champagne problem, or something that might happen in the future once we've succeeded at overcoming other hurdles. I often hear start-up founders worrying about their site crashing after launch. To that I say, "Congratulations!" If that were to happen, it would mean they had created a great product that people truly wanted. That is the hardest part!

After my first big failure, I learned to focus better on what mattered in the moment, and to worry about tomorrow's problems tomorrow. For ClassPass, that meant getting people to class even if we had to stay up until 4 a.m. to input reservations manually. Processing any reservation meant more than raising more money, getting more press, or fancy dinners and events. This was the key to ClassPass's magic. This was our purpose.

As another example, not too long after we launched, when we were a company of six people, we ran a promotion in which we gave away a Lululemon gift card. We had a few hundred customers, and we needed more. We didn't have any formal partnership with Lululemon. We simply purchased gift cards from their website and gave them to a customer when they redeemed their membership.

The old me would never have done this. I would have been immobilized by doubt and worry over our lack of a formal corporate partnership. I probably wouldn't have even done the promo until this was worked out. But the new me lived by a different mantra. I forged ahead, knowing that fear and doubt are only constructs in the mind—and understanding that if this resulted in a misstep, I'd learn from it and move on.

It worked. The Lululemon gift card was an effective incentive to get people to sign up, and we grew to about a thousand customers. Then, about three to four months after launching the promotion, we heard from Lululemon in the form of a cease-and-desist letter, demanding we stop using their name. Of course, no one wants to receive a legal threat, but the new me popped the champagne. Lululemon knew who we were!

This business lesson reflects a philosophy that I now apply to my entire life. I no longer make a huge deal about every little detail, and I don't let my worry about what might happen in the future stifle me. I have learned to figure things out as they come and focus on what's most important versus trying to solve for every option from the beginning. There will always be missteps, obstacles, and failures along the way, and we can never predict what all those will be. So we can either let that freeze us in fear so that we don't do anything, or we can simply move forward, even taking risks—despite our doubts.

Fear and doubt are
only in my mind.

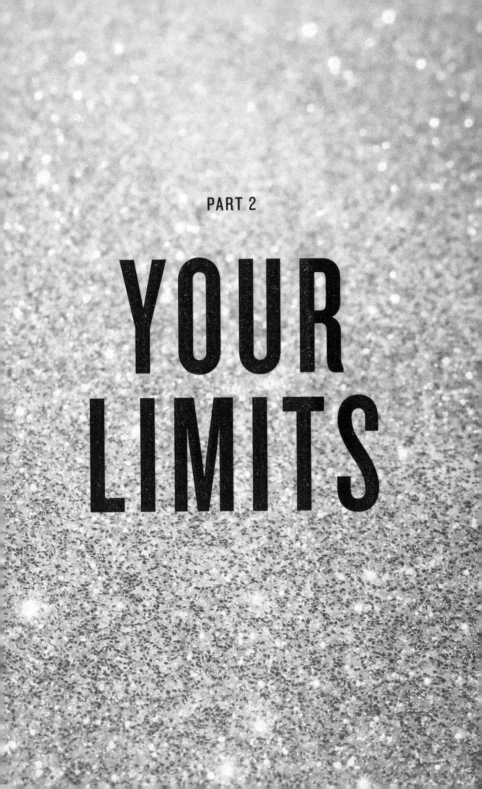

PART 2

YOUR
LIMITS

5

FINANCES

What is money worth to you?

THE SIGHT OF MY DAD HUNCHED over a spreadsheet, absorbed in numbers, was a familiar scene. But this time it was different. My dad, forever the financial planner in our family, had offered to help me put together a budget to see whether I had the personal financial resources to start a company. I knew I wanted to start a company, but *could* I?

I had already conjured up the courage and confidence to quit my job, but I would need to forgo a salary while I launched ClassPass. This meant no income. While I had been meticulously saving for the past number of years, and cutting my spending down to the necessities, was that enough to still pay my bills and live in New York City? And if so, for how long?

I didn't know it at the time, but that piece of paper—and everything that went into it—was my ticket to freedom.

Finally, after what seemed like an insanely long period of silence, my dad looked up from the spreadsheet splayed out in front of him. "Okay, Payal, this gives me a good idea of what you're dealing with."

I was nervous as he summed it up, but also eager—I knew that what I needed even more than money was information. I needed to understand and quantify the risk of starting ClassPass and my financial constraints. At the time, I had no idea how much money I would be able to raise to start the company, and when (or if) those funds would allow me to take a salary. I needed a solid plan that would allow me to meet my responsibilities while pursuing my dreams. I had so many questions: *How long will it take for the company to launch? Can I afford to stay in my apartment? Will I need to find other sources of income?*

My dad continued: "I think if you keep your expenses to within twenty-five hundred dollars a month, you have enough of a cushion to go three years without taking a salary." This was great news, not just because it showed that I could take the leap, but also because it proved that the sacrifices I'd been making for years had been worth it.

I'm not sure if it's nurture or nature, but I have always been a saver. It was in part because I had to be. Growing up, we didn't have a lot of money. My parents had always carefully budgeted, making every dollar they earned stretch as far as possible. My father was a chemist at Colgate-Palmolive. His salary paid for our home and expenses, of course, but outside of these necessities, he was laser focused on providing my sister and me with the best possible education. My parents scrimped and saved so they could afford to move to a new house just a mile away from our first home so we could attend the best public schools in New Jersey. In addition to cooking and cleaning, my mother worked multiple jobs to add to our family savings. She worked harder than anyone I've ever known. This instilled in us the true value of a dollar and what it meant to attach a purpose to money. I was taught not to spend frivolously. Going to the mall to shop for fun with friends wasn't something I experienced. My family went shopping for clothes at Kmart at the beginning of the school year. My sister and I were given a budget and had to figure out how to make it work.

My parents taught me that the first step to financial freedom was planning how to budget, save, and spend, and knowing the numbers inside and out. As a child, I inherited or absorbed their penchant for saving and started a coin collection, which I added to whenever I found spare change.

I started saving as soon as I started working. I didn't know exactly what I was saving for, but as with my childhood coin collection, I simply socked away portions of each paycheck. I could have spent money on new clothes, trips, and eating out, but I knew that there was a larger purpose for this money.

Now I knew what it was: becoming an entrepreneur. Sitting with my dad in the kitchen, I looked at the three-year budget he'd created. *Okay,* I thought with the confidence that only numbers and facts can provide. *I can do this.* By budgeting and saving, and now planning, I had bought myself three years of freedom. I had earned the ability to follow my dreams.

We don't often talk about money and purpose in the same breath. It's as if the very idea of purpose is too lofty to be tainted by money. But we live in the real world where money is essential. To have the freedom and confidence to chase our purpose, we have to address our finances. So ask yourself: *Is money holding me back from pursuing my dreams?* If the answer is yes, it's time to make some changes and create a plan. This is your life, and you get to decide what money is worth and what is most valuable to you. How much does it cost to do what you love?

MONEY AND HOW TO MAKE THE MOST OF IT

In 2010, when I was twenty-seven years old and still working at Warner, I laid everything on the line—from my reputation to my savings—for Sa's weekend-long Premiere NYC Showcase. I had done smaller showcases (including the studio showcase I described earlier), but putting this event together was by far the biggest thing I had done in my life up to that point. Just to reserve the theater I had to put down twenty thousand dollars—all the money in my savings account, and there was no guarantee that I'd get a single penny of it back.

It was on me to sell enough tickets to break even. I didn't even think about making a profit. And of course, there were tons of other costs beyond the initial deposit: I had four separate costumes made in India for each of the dancers; I'd hired a lighting designer and stage manager; and then there were marketing costs and programs to print. The list went on and on. After meticulously setting a budget, I knew that I had to sell a thousand tickets to cover my costs. That was an intimidating number.

The Saturday before the show, I was at rehearsal with the rest of the troupe and Usha Aunty. She had come to take over for me as director for the final week so that I could focus on my own performance instead of fretting about other details. But that day, I was distracted by constant pings from my phone.

When we finally took a break, I checked my messages and saw that I had received dozens of texts from people all asking if I could get them tickets.

At first, I was confused because the tickets were easily accessible online. Then I realized that they were trying to call in favors because all three shows had sold out! I immediately felt relieved to know that the financial risk I had taken was now absolved. I was also flooded with an incredible sense of validation for pursuing my passion, along with a strong sense of responsibility to make my community proud.

We opened that show with a traditional performance–based Garba dance, which I have always loved. As we began to dance, my fears and worries about the show melted away and were replaced by the pure joy of performing. At the end, when the audience rose to their feet, I knew that what I was feeling alongside the rest of the dancers had extended from the stage to every seat in the theater. As we took our bows, I thought about how hard we had all worked for that moment. I wasn't a theater person or a producer, but I had put together an entire show and executed my dream. There had been so many risks and unknowns along the way, but I realized that if I could pull off this show, there was more I could do in life if the outcome was important enough to me. This experience—of developing a saving habit, and then using that money to fund my dreams—made me feel secure enough to take an even bigger risk when I started my own company.

Financial independence is in many ways a luxury and privilege. Having a cushion to invest in something we believe in is neither something that everyone can afford nor something that can be accomplished overnight. However, it's also more within reach than many people think. Wherever you are starting from, following the steps in this chapter can help you become more financially free, starting today.

The first step is to identify your personal relationship with money. Start by asking yourself: *What does money mean to me?* This is a big question that can be difficult to approach since everyone's experience is so unique. Our upbringing, our lifestyle, and the messaging we receive from our family and community all impact our understanding of money and how we value it.

Some of us are taught to save at all costs. Others learn to let money ebb and flow more fluidly. Money is literally worth different things to different people, so there is no right or wrong way to spend it—as long as we don't put our own or our family's safety and security at risk.

To help understand your own relationship with money, think about the role money played in your childhood. How did your parents relate to money? What were their spending habits, and how did they affect your opportunities when you were growing up? As an adult, have you replicated your parents' relationship with money in your own life? Or have you intentionally carved out your own unique or different approach?

Next, consider the role that money currently plays in your life. Is it simply funding your lifestyle? Is it something you're constantly worried about? Do you feel you never have enough? In what ways do you already use money to create the life you most want? Think about this honestly and without judgment. For now, simply identify how you feel about money and your saving and spending habits. Knowing this, it will be easier to adjust your habits in whatever ways are necessary to fund what really matters.

WHAT IS MONEY WORTH TO YOU?

Since money is a critical factor in all major life decisions, take a moment to examine your relationship with it. Take stock of your everyday choices, now and at different points in your life, and note what you choose to spend money on. Also identify other values besides money. To explore the role money plays in your life, answer the following questions:

1   How do you regard money? Is it a means to an end, a symbol of success, or something else? Is not having enough an obstacle?

2   What are you getting out of your job besides money? Fulfillment? Flexibility? Skills? Connections? These also have value. What are these worth compared to financial rewards?

3   To what extent do you spend money on what you care about? What experiences or physical products mean something to you?

Understanding your feelings about money will help you prioritize your spending in a way that supports your life goals, especially when it's time to create a budget that truly works for you.

KNOW YOUR NUMBERS

Do you have a clear picture of your current financial situation? To pursue your life goals and move forward with confidence, you must know your numbers, or your financial starting point.

Almost everyone has limited resources, so to keep money from holding you back from your goals, planning is essential. I cannot stress enough the importance of setting a budget and tracking your progress. This is something that can neither be ignored nor outsourced.

A big mistake I've seen people make is outsourcing budgeting to someone else, whether it's their spouse, a parent, a business manager, or an accountant. It's fine to seek help—I sure did—but make sure you know what's going on with your money. This is especially true for women. Feeling dependent on anyone else takes away from your freedom. It's important to understand your finances and play a role in decision-making. You have to know how your money already flows in order to make any necessary adjustments to reach your goals.

Whether or not you are the breadwinner in your family, you should have your pulse on all the family finances. This is the only way to live comfortably and make confident decisions. Information is power.

If you are married or have a partner you share financial responsibilities with, it's also important to understand each other's relationship with money and your joint financial picture. It's helpful to know what each person is trying to accomplish with finances. This can help reduce frustration when or if your partner doesn't spend money in the same ways you do. It's important to collectively discuss and track progress, so you both feel financially supported to do what you love.

Further, consider what financial responsibilities you have to others. When budgeting, this often means focusing on debts— such as credit cards, student loans, mortgages, and so on. However, also keep in mind the other people who depend on you, such as a partner, parents, kids, and others. As I've said, my parents felt responsible to pay for their children's education, and they planned for those expenses their whole lives. Are there expenses down the road that you should plan for now, or temporary expenses, such as caring for a parent, that you need to maintain?

Then, consider your essential expenses—the things you must cover in order to maintain your current life. This includes your rent or mortgage, utility bills, car payments, insurance, groceries, debts, childcare expenses, and so on.

Finally, consider all the other things you spend money on. Do you get coffee from a café every morning? Do you have a standing lunch date with a friend? How often do you buy new clothes, take a trip, or impulse shop? Often, we don't even realize how much mindless spending we do on a whim or for personal enjoyment. Look back at receipts and credit card bills to jog your memory and see exactly where your money is going. It can be overwhelming to see how much you spend in black and white, but you can't manage what you don't measure.

I always feel more confident and in control of my life when I know the numbers. It gives me the freedom to take chances on the things I want while also making sure I preserve my responsibilities. If you don't have this in one place already, write it all down on a spreadsheet that covers at least a month, and maybe more. Many online tools and apps make it easy. Personally, I track everything I spend on websites and apps like Mint. However you do it, make tracking your finances a regular practice, so you never have to wonder where the money is going.

BUDGETING AND PRIORITIES

Whatever you want to achieve in life will most likely impact your finances, since it will require more time, more money, or both. Ultimately, we need to be disciplined about budgeting in order to afford our dreams and reach our potential. Whether we want to save money to go to school, to quit our job and start our own company, or to support a creative project, money doesn't have to be a constraint if we plan ahead. Budgeting to support our priorities is the way to buy ourselves freedom.

This is why it's important to understand your current financial picture. From this, you can plot out a new budget that supports your priorities and dreams. Look at your list of expenses and consider which could be cut back. If you want to spend more money for a new goal, are there areas where you can reduce spending to compensate? Remember, you are in control of these trade-offs, and there are no right or wrong answers. Everyone has their own opinion about which expenses are essential and which are unnecessary or expendable. The point is to prioritize what matters to you. Don't work for your money, make your money work for you.

When I was trying to reduce my spending, I slashed my costs down to what I considered were the essentials. I lived in a rental apartment in Manhattan with my sister in a flex room the size of a closet. I walked to work and to dance rehearsal instead of paying for cabs or subway fare. I limited nonessential expenses like clothing and travel as much as possible.

When potential expenses came up, I always asked myself: *What does this dinner or dress or trip mean to me?* Don't get me wrong; I didn't say no to everything! But I evaluated everything to make sure what I was getting in exchange for my money was worthwhile.

For example, I once received an invite to a close friend's bachelorette party. I knew this would be an expensive event, much more than I'd ordinarily spend, but our friendship and this experience were too important to me, so I made room in my budget to attend.

Even when I was budgeting to the extreme, I never felt like I was sacrificing too much, since I was able to spend on what I decided was important. That, in and of itself, is a true luxury. By being strategic about saving, I was able to afford what might have once seemed prohibitively expensive. Most of all, I always compared whatever I was choosing to do without to what the money I was saving would let me afford. When we are choosing to sacrifice for our dreams, it often doesn't feel like a sacrifice at all.

Another thing to keep in mind is that it's important not to get distracted or influenced by other people's habits around money. Sometimes seeing how our friends, family members, and neighbors are spending their money can affect our own financial values. Don't compare yourself to others, and keep your mind clear of other people's judgments. Simply be honest with yourself about what *you* need to live a truly fulfilling life.

Remember not to chase what others have.
Know what money means to you and more
importantly the freedom it can provide.
When you think about the kind of life you want,
consider what it will cost and what you need.

MAKE YOUR MONEY WORK FOR YOU

Once you have a sense of your financial picture, it's important to start thinking about ways you can make your money support your goals. This might involve changes with how you're spending, saving, and investing your money.

1   Are there certain things you'd like to spend more on? Or save toward?

2   Are there certain things you spend money on that you could spend less on if you had to?

3   If you needed to, are there potential ways you could secure extra cash? If so, what and how much?

Reflect on your answers. In part 3, the goal-setting section, we will come up with a plan to actionably move these numbers in the direction you'd like.

RISK CALCULATION

Too often, lack of money is a constraint that keeps us from reaching our potential. Finances must be a consideration when following our dreams, but this does not mean we should live in fear of risk. I like to think of risk as an opportunity that will lead down a new path. But that only happens if we properly plan.

Risk and calculation go hand-in-hand, as do responsibilities and dreams. We shouldn't make a big move such as quitting our job, starting a company, or chasing our dreams if we haven't taken the necessary steps to become financially stable. To do otherwise is careless. We undermine our chances of success if we don't calculate the costs and the risks, and if we don't balance following our dreams with our responsibilities. At a minimum, being worried and distracted will only take away from our ability to focus on succeeding in what we want.

You may be in a situation where a major shift isn't practical. Perhaps, for a variety of reasons, you want to remain in your current job. If this is the case, it makes sense to assess your skills and consider finding a side hustle that can help supplement your income. In our current gig economy, there are so many opportunities for side jobs, and many people from all walks of life pursue them. Side hustles do more than put extra money in your pocket; they can help you gain or hone a skill that's connected to your calling or introduce you to someone who might be instrumental on your path.

In the very early stages of starting ClassPass, when I wasn't taking a salary, I was making good use of the gig economy to help further stretch my financial cushion. I gave private bridal dance sessions, taught a few dance classes, and did freelance consulting work for a digital marketing organization. Further, each of those jobs helped me develop more transferable skills. When I was consulting for a nonprofit arts organization, I learned about email marketing and how to build a subscriber list and increase click-throughs. I only spent about twenty hours a month on this project, yet the experience and skills I gained proved incredibly useful when I began marketing ClassPass.

Every month, I returned to my budget and assessed whether I needed to increase my earnings by raising my rates or adding another side hustle. In most cases, just knowing the numbers empowered me and clarified the best next step without feeling like I was heading down the wrong path. By understanding the data, I had the agency to make real yet calculated strides toward my calling.

Risk calculation also involves evaluating the trade-off between time and money. I had to be careful about how many hours I spent on these freelance jobs, which were meant to earn money, versus the hours I had available to build my company. In time, after I had enough investor interest and buzz around the company, I shifted the balance, so that I gave up some income to spend more time going all-in on ClassPass.

At this point I switched my mentality from one of saving to one of growth. Now that I was truly doing what I loved, capitalizing on my time became more important than reducing all of my costs. I didn't have time for a one-hour walk home from work to save money. A fifteen-dollar cab ride saved me forty-five minutes, which I could use to work on my start-up plans. This is another aspect of risk calculation to keep in mind: When is it wiser to maximize saving money, and when is it wiser to maximize your time? Both have value, and sometimes, the investment in time can provide exponentially greater benefits than hoarding a few more dollars. Neither mindset is inherently better than the other, so simply be aware of which mindset you are in, and switch as circumstances change.

In terms of time, the biggest issue is often how much flexibility your current work allows for you to pursue your calling at the same time. Some jobs afford plenty, and some none at all—and to truly pursue your dreams, you might eventually need to change your employment situation. If that seems like the case for you, recognize it and plan for it. Start budgeting and saving today and building up your financial resources, while also calculating how much time and energy you need for your passion to thrive. Prepare for the day when you take the full leap.

THE KEY TO A RICH LIFE

When I first went to Silicon Valley to raise money, the response to our pitches was radio silence. Then, once ClassPass proved itself as a viable model in multiple cities, VCs started courting us! I had VCs offer to take me out to dinner, to sporting events, and to meet other partners in their firms. This felt great, but I was wary. If these investors hadn't deemed me worthy of taking a bet on before, would they feel that way again? Financing deals happen at warp speed. At one point, I had twenty-four hours to decide who to take an investment from. The stakes were high. I knew that whoever I signed a deal with would end up with some level of control over the company.

The obvious choice would have been to sign with a big-name VC firm, which would give us money and credibility. But I wasn't comfortable letting someone who hadn't been interested in me from the beginning take ownership of my vision now. I wanted to make sure the right people were around the table—ones who believed in me.

So I did what some people might consider unthinkable—I said no to top VCs and turned down their offers. Instead, I chose Fritz Lanman, an angel investor who had led my seed round of financing and had been working closely with me and the team from the beginning. I knew Fritz saw value in what we were doing, and he would be a true partner who would support me and ClassPass's vision. That was worth more to me than all the money in the world.

I'll never forget the morning that ClassPass announced the funding round that brought the company's valuation to over one billion dollars. In business, this valuation earns a start-up "unicorn" status. At the time, being eight months pregnant with my first child made it feel even more special. I spent the day doing interviews and answering the same question over and over again: "What does this unicorn status mean to you?"

This raises another issue when it comes to money and meaning, though it's another champagne problem. Ideally, we will experience success as we pursue our calling, and this might well involve financial rewards, increased status or fame, or whatever standard is used to measure progress in our field. This is something to celebrate, but it can also become a distraction, a false sign of success. We need to remember that the richest people in the world are not the ones earning the most money, the ones with the biggest houses and nicest cars. The richest people are the ones who are fulfilled. Maintaining that sense of fulfillment is an ongoing effort, one that continues even as we experience success.

Of course, I was honored by the accolades and attention, especially since ClassPass was one of just a handful of start-ups founded by a woman to reach that milestone. In those interviews, however, I kept emphasizing that the magic of our company was not the billion-dollar valuation. I was most proud of the hustle of my team and the impact we had on people's lives—the hundreds of millions of reservations we booked, the new experiences people gained. I had learned throughout my entrepreneurial journey, and especially through fundraising, that I couldn't let money change my vision—or change me.

Growth and success are great; they validate our vision and provide the resources to keep going. But growth needs to happen in ways that support our original vision and goals. This is where developing the ongoing practice of establishing budgets and financial plans, both monthly and annually, can help. As you set and reach certain milestones, you can anticipate exactly how much money (and other resources) you need to get to the next step. This way, growth happens in a way that supports what you love, rather than veers away from it. Remember, purpose and calling give us something that dollars can't.

I don't work for money;
money works for me.

6

SKILLS

What do you bring to the table?

I'VE NEVER CONSIDERED MYSELF A NATURAL-BORN salesperson, and that's fine—except when it became a requirement to get ClassPass off the ground. When the company's success depended on me getting boutique gyms and studios on board, I was nervous. Despite my passion, I was not confident in my ability to sell it to others. For one thing, I didn't have any professional sales experience. Sure, there was no shortage of theories and training programs on how to be good at sales, but I had no experience with any of them! I had, however, taken hundreds of dance classes.

Not sure how to get a foot in the door of these boutique fitness studios, I did what seemed obvious. I walked in their doors . . . and took a class. The summer we launched, along with other members of the early team, I took four to five classes a day—sprinting from the office to a yoga studio in midtown to a barre class on the Upper East Side to a Pilates reformer studio in Brooklyn and then to a dance class downtown. It was exhausting, but I found being tired calmed my nerves. It helped me approach studio owners and served as a better excuse for my sweating than anxiety!

More than that, participating in classes firsthand helped me and others on the team connect with studio owners directly, since the owners were often the instructors. Once the class was over, we waited in the studio's lobby, and when the owner emerged, we made our pitch for ClassPass. On an iPad, we showed them what we were doing and how it worked for the studios and students. We tried to have a conversation about the owner's business, listened to their needs, and then shared our story. Instead of trying to "sell" in those meetings, I focused on being myself. After all, I was a lifelong dancer and enthusiastic class taker, and I wholeheartedly wanted to help get more people to class. I believed in what I was saying. Studio owners saw that, and they saw the value in partnering with us.

Soon, I found myself closing deals with most of the studios I spoke with. When I first started, I didn't think I'd be able to sign anyone because of my lack of formal sales experience and training. But by turning sales into a personal moment, I learned that I did have the ability to sell.

This chapter explores skills. It helps you identify the ones you already have and the ones you need to acquire in order to accomplish your goals. Oftentimes, people tell me they feel like they don't have the right skills or experience to accomplish what they want. That's how they *feel*, but that's not usually the reality. People often possess more skills and abilities than they realize, and they can acquire any others that they need, so rather than feeling held back, they make themselves ready to spring into action.

BUILDING FOUNDATIONAL SKILLS

As you know, my family values education and preparedness. So it may seem surprising that I started ClassPass without any of the background most people would expect me to have. I never went to business school. I never worked in the fitness industry. I had never been involved in a start-up. Yet, when I left my corporate job to pursue ClassPass full-time, I knew in my heart that I was (mostly) ready.

While I value education and believe developing foundational skills is paramount, I've also learned that acquiring skills can happen in different ways, and skills are transferable. Our unique life experience provides us with many skills that, even if they seem unrelated, can be applied directly to our calling.

For example, in high school, I worked at a telemarketing research agency. I spent two months every summer calling up people and asking them survey questions. At first, I was shy and nervous when talking to adults. Soon, though, I realized that I had an advantage when talking to people over the phone versus face to face. If I used my voice to connect with the person on the other end of the line, I could transcend anything that made me feel different and insecure. Instead of just launching into the surveys, I started by spending a few minutes getting to know the person on the other end of the phone. I asked how their day was going or a question about where they lived. As a teenager living in the Northeast, I was fascinated to learn about life in other parts of the country. And when these people sensed my genuine curiosity, they were more likely to engage with me—though of course, some still hung up.

This was one of my first experiences putting myself in other people's shoes instead of focusing on my own agenda. I found that the more I did this, the more my confidence grew when speaking to people in different situations. I learned how to connect authentically with people. As a shy high schooler, this made me more confident. From this minimum-wage telemarketing job, which had nothing to do with my life purpose, I was introduced to some of the foundational skills of selling that helped me, as an adult, fulfill my purpose.

These skills have served me well throughout my career. Being able to foster empowering conversations is valuable in almost any context. At Bain, they called me "the queen of cold calling" because of these skills. While I was initially anxious about selling studio owners on ClassPass, since I had no sales training, I discovered that my conversational abilities transferred. Do not underestimate the value of a summer gig!

I have picked up transferable skills from everything I've done in life. From my education and training at MIT, I learned how to solve problems. At Bain, I learned how to become an instant expert on different industries, which helped me understand and strategize various aspects of my own business as we evolved ClassPass's business model. At Warner, I watched the entire music industry shift from physical to digital media, which was incredibly helpful as ClassPass was redesigning another industry—the fitness industry. And of course, building Sa Dance Company helped prepare me to create, build, and market an entire company. The skills I gained made me a better entrepreneur and leader.

Everything we learn from every stage of our life provides us with real-world experience we can use to achieve our goals.

Even an unfulfilling job can teach critical skills that we can use to succeed at what we love. If your current situation isn't what you ultimately want to be doing, don't dismiss that experience, since it may one day serve you and your calling. Collect all the knowledge and experience possible to make yourself ready for the next stage in your journey. Pay attention to everything you are learning and all the skills you are using and developing. How might you apply those things as you move forward toward your goals?

WHAT DO YOU BRING TO THE TABLE?

SELF-CHECK POINT

Our skills are cultivated through every job and experience, and those skills can transfer to your purpose-driven work.

To explore your existing skills, write down five activities that have been a regular part of your day-to-day work life, either currently or in the past. Next to each task, write down a specific skill that has helped you succeed at that task. Here are some examples to get you started:

Making lots of calls   COMMUNICATION SKILLS

Giving presentations   PUBLIC SPEAKING

Creating spreadsheets   SYNTHESIZING NEW INFORMATION

Doing research   ANALYZING

Motivating a team   LEADERSHIP SKILLS

> Review the list of skills. Do any stand out or surprise you? Are there any secondary or related skills that you've overlooked and could name? Consider how these skills might be applied to what you need to do to succeed at your dreams. And from now on, be aware of any new skills you are gaining from any job or project. Keep track of your building blocks as you work toward charting your own path.

FOLLOW YOUR OWN PATTERNS OF SUCCESS

When starting ClassPass, I quickly discovered that one skill I seemed to lack was fundraising. We did not raise a dollar from our first round of VC meetings.

While venting to a fellow Techstars founder, he helped me process the problem in a more productive way.

"Payal, you've clearly succeeded in your life, or you wouldn't be in this program," he said. "What are other environments that have made you feel more confident?"

"Onstage performing," I said, without thinking.

"Okay, so how do you get ready for a show?" he asked.

"Oh, that's easy," I said. "I practice lots and focus on the story I'm trying to convey."

"Well, why would you do these meetings any differently?" he asked.

Wow. He was right. Why was I doing the complete opposite?

I had an image of how these pitch meetings should go, what a founder should look like, and even what a founder should wear. In my mind, it was all very corporate, professional, and cookie cutter. For these meetings, I put on the old suits I had worn when I worked at Bain, though I never really felt comfortable wearing them. Once again, I felt insecure about my height, but instead of owning it—as I had years ago when I stayed seated for that job interview—I tried to compensate in other ways. I memorized my talking points, and I focused completely on making sure I could explain every number on my spreadsheets. I heard myself speaking robotically and nervously, and I could feel a lack of connection. It's no wonder it didn't work. How could an investor like me? I didn't like me! I was awkward and impersonal. But I thought I was doing what I was supposed to—look professional, sound professional, know the facts.

Now I had the key. Despite that disclaimer on mutual funds, I've found that past performance *is* an indicator of future results. I connected back to my own method of preparation, which I knew how to execute and perform well. I thought about how to transform those meetings into a performance environment. I asked myself: *If this were a performance, what would I do differently? How would I think about my audience, and what would I want them to take away?*

For example, when I was choreographing a new show, I always focused on the story I wanted to tell and how I hoped the work would make the audience feel. That guided my choices. When it came to potential investors, I wanted them to feel a connection to my passion and to see I had the right skills to execute my vision. I wanted them to feel without a doubt that I was the right person to invest in. At this stage in the process, I knew they were investing in me above all else. Finding this clarity was a huge moment for me. All I had to do was choreograph my "performance" to elicit the response I wanted. I had to inject that magic into my presentations, and I identified preparation, storytelling, and passion as the keystones to my success.

I realized I had been dreading these meetings, which led me to approach them all wrong. Instead, I needed to be just as excited as before any dance performance. For the next investor meeting, I left my suit at the dry cleaners. I showed up in my black leggings, which I always felt most comfortable in. And before I dove into the numbers, spreadsheets, and slides, I told the investors my story of learning to dance as a young girl and how hard I had fought to keep dance in my life as an adult.

Soon, my pitches were more like actual performances. I told a story, expressed my feelings, and fed off the energy of the people in the room. In those later meetings, the version of me that came alive onstage was teleported into the glass-walled offices. I even started looking forward to the meetings! The irony was that, once I was finally at ease, I didn't have to do it anymore. When it came time to raise money for our second round of VC funding, a venture capitalist told me, "You don't have to come in for a partner meeting again. We know you. We're in."

Take a moment to think back on your own life, to something you had to work hard for and succeeded at getting. How did you do it? What was your pattern of success? Those same skills and patterns will work in any environment. Some people succeed when learning from others or in a group. Other people do better alone. Some people succeed when they understand an entire problem before trying to tackle it. Others have more success by figuring things out as they go along. Have you been in a situation where you had to think on your feet and solve problems? How did you handle it?

This same thing applies to leadership. Pursuing your vision will require being a leader, but if that feels unfamiliar or uncomfortable, consider any type of situation in which you have worked with and overseen other people: in a committee, a school group, or even during a family vacation. How do you typically work with others to get tasks done? When challenges have come up, how do you keep everyone working toward the ultimate goal? Whatever your answer, use the same skills that have worked before to get things done.

MAP YOUR PATTERNS OF SUCCESS

SELF-CHECK POINT

You can take the skills learned in past situations—formal and informal—and apply them to your calling. To start figuring out your own patterns of success, answer the following questions:

1 Think of a recent accomplishment whether personal, professional, formal, or informal.

2 What were the circumstances (key players, environment, skills) that you believe helped you succeed?

3 What were the challenges you faced while working toward that goal, and how did you overcome them?

Do this review of other significant experiences, especially whenever you're feeling stifled in your abilities. The answer you need may exist within a past pattern of success.

THE POWER OF PRACTICE

One of the investors who decided to fund our start-up was Silicon Valley venture capitalist Adam Valkin. And he did it for an interesting reason: He saw me dance.

In my initial meeting with Adam, as I shared my story and background, he asked me to show him a video of a dance performance, which I was happy to do. Adam is a serious tennis player—he played on the varsity team at Harvard—and he understands the hard work and discipline it takes to perform physically at a high level. He also understands what it takes to create a show involving many dancers. That video gave him the information he needed to take a bet on me. It was something that I couldn't explain in a pitch meeting; it was something he had to see.

Afterward, when Adam joined us for meetings with other potential investors, he routinely did something that I found amusing. At some point during the introductions, Adam would interrupt and say, "Hold on, I need to show you something." He would then take out his phone and show a video of me dancing. He explained that was why he had invested. "If you can be that good at this," he said, "I know you can be that good at anything."

Producing good work is the result of hard work. Of practice. Of mastery. Steve Martin once said, "Be so good they can't ignore you," and I have adopted that as my philosophy. As a petite Indian woman and the baby of my family, I have always felt like the underdog who must prove herself. For me, this started early. When I was a little girl training with Usha Aunty, each girl in our dance group was placed in position in order of skill. I was always the fourth girl on the left. There was nothing wrong with being fourth in line, but I was determined to work my way up.

Our group would gather every Saturday in one of our basements and practice a single step over and over until we all had it down. Then we had to show up the next week having practiced and perfected the step. Rehearsing on my own helped, but learning this level of discipline in class as a group was transformative. The other girls and I operated as a unit, and the shapes we made in formation had to be perfect. Measuring the distance between each of us required precision and awareness, especially when we were simultaneously moving around the stage. We had to think about the angle of our arm, since a centimeter too high or too low wouldn't cut it! Each of us aimed to achieve proficiency so that we would never be the one to mess it up for everyone else. This took hours of practice.

I also wanted to have those steps memorized in my muscles so when it was time to perform, I would be able to completely let go. This meant mastering the art of discipline so I could unleash myself to be the best performer I could be. I rehearsed (and rehearsed *and rehearsed*) so that the movements were in my body and nothing could throw me when I was onstage. By the time I was in Usha Aunty's senior group, my hard work had paid off and I was the first girl on the left.

Maybe the most important skill, and the one that is also the most transferable, is discipline. Mastering the fundamentals through the power of practice. This enables growth and fuels creativity. It means understanding something innately, so that it becomes second nature, which allows us to perform at the highest levels. This doesn't have to be a physical discipline. It can be achieving a deep-rooted understanding of a subject, so that you become an expert and know the topic inside and out.

> *Achieving expertise or mastery is the result*
> *of discipline and hard work. No one reaches*
> *a high level through talent or smarts alone.*
> *In fact, the inner drive to be the best is often*
> *the most important factor in success.*

And as Adam expressed, if we can demonstrate the discipline to achieve mastery in one area, we can do so with anything we put our mind to. The range of skills we learn from the power of practice can be applied to any situation.

Take a moment to think about something you have worked hard for in the past. It doesn't have to be related to work or school. I strongly believe that training in anything is training in everything. Did you give your all to a sport or hobby? Did you dedicate yourself to becoming a better parent, partner, or friend?

Ultimately, whether you succeeded or not, whether you became the best, doesn't matter. What truly counts is developing the drive, passion, and perseverance to work hard through every obstacle.

When people see that, they will reward you for it. Some of my first investors, the friends and family who offered me checks, told me that they gave me money because they knew about my dedication to dance, or they saw the Sa show and understood what I could accomplish if I set my mind to it. They believed I would be able to do it again. Past performance does indicate future results!

A BIAS FOR ACTION

Another skill that is not commonly thought of as a skill is the ability to execute. While we want to be as prepared as possible before we do something, we also can't wait until conditions are perfect before moving forward. Once we identify our purpose and goals, we need to take action to make them real. In a way, this relates to risk calculation. Sometimes, if we don't act now, time might slip away and we will lose our opportunity. In other words, don't underestimate the importance of hustle!

An example of this arose when other companies started copying ClassPass. Once we had proven our ideas worked in a few cities and raised capital, competitors popped up in other markets that were exact replicas of our website. When we would change our site, they would change their site. It was a land grab in every city, and I found it incredibly frustrating. I always believed we should focus on our company and future and not the competition, but at one point it seemed like every email I opened said, "Have you heard of this new service in Austin?" or "Did you see this ClassPass knockoff in Atlanta?"

Reading these emails, sometimes late at night, I felt anxious. Some of these new entrants were former venture capitalists. They had access to capital and connections. And thanks to ClassPass and our years of hard work, they had a proven model. Then I remembered we had something else, our mission, which was our gold. This was our idea, and no one could replicate that.

However, I realized we needed to move faster. We needed to act. This was fall 2014, and our plan was to open in one city a month for the rest of the year. That wasn't going to be enough.

I knew whoever executed first in a new city had the best chance to win the market. To protect ourselves, we needed more cities, and fast!

Some people advised that I sue my competitors, but I knew that wasn't the right choice. We would lose time by getting tied up in the courts. Instead, we went on the offensive and launched an internal project called "Operation 2015." Our plan was to open in fifteen additional cities over the last three months of the year, so that we totaled twenty cities , instead of our originally planned eight cities, by January 1, 2015.

Did I know how to do that? No, of course not! But I didn't have time to figure it out before starting to act. We put ads on Craigslist and hired thirty salespeople over a weekend; after a day of prep, we flew them to various US cities armed with our playbook. We started the year with less than ten employees. We ended it with close to one hundred. By January, ClassPass was officially in twenty markets.

Executing requires making hard decisions. There was no guarantee our plan would work. While I don't know what would have happened if we'd stuck with our original plan and only opened in eight cities by January 2015, I know ClassPass wouldn't have become what it has. I've learned that with attention, focus, and a bias for action, we can achieve more than we think is possible.

ALWAYS KEEP GROWING

As the story above illustrates, we don't always feel ready for the challenges that arise, and sometimes our original plans need to be tossed out the window. Being successful can often depend on how flexible, adaptable, and courageous we are in the moment, and how open we are to learning and growing in whatever ways are necessary. No one pursues their calling already knowing everything they need to know or possessing all the necessary skills. But by taking action and hitting dead ends, by learning from failures and trying again, we learn what skills and knowledge we're missing, and we can close that gap. We shouldn't put our dreams on hold because we aren't completely ready. Instead, we can take action, even if it's just small steps, and learn through doing.

Some of the most impressive people I've met are a perfect combination of confident and curious. Throughout my dance career and as the founder of ClassPass, I have witnessed firsthand what continuous discovery and learning can do for people. That's part of the promise of ClassPass and what our members want—the opportunities to learn new skills, push their bodies further, and grow mentally. The hardest part for most people is starting, just getting to that first class or lesson. Fear often holds people back.

I experienced this firsthand. The truth is, I was never a fitness person. I had never worked out other than the training I did for dance. I didn't own a pair of sneakers until my twenties! When I went to a yoga class, I was intimidated by the flexibility of those around me, and in my first spin classes, I didn't even know how to clip in the shoes! Recognizing how scared I was to take new classes—and how most people can be scared to try something new—allowed me to empathize and connect with the ClassPass customer. I understood the value of helping others get over the fear of trying new things. Being an outsider to the fitness industry also allowed me to think entirely differently about it—and not be afraid to do something different. Approach life with confidence and curiosity, with

7

PEOPLE

Who will aid you on your journey?

BY THE FALL OF 2015, CLASSPASS was expanding throughout the United States and globally at a rapid pace. Once again, I wanted to share with my parents something new that I was working on, so that they felt part of my journey. My husband, Nick, and I took them out to dinner in Manhattan for a joint birthday celebration—my parents were born three days apart! After we left the restaurant, instead of going right back to my apartment, we made a surprise detour. On Seventh Avenue, I led them past the security desk and into the marble lobby of an office building, and we took the elevator up to the eleventh floor. When the elevator doors opened, there was a giant ClassPass sign—the letters created out of sneaker laces filling the wall.

Up until this point, the ClassPass team had been working in makeshift offices around New York City. We were strewn across different buildings and random floors, but now for the first time we could all be together in a single office. My excitement was especially heightened that night, since the next morning, the hundreds of empty desks would be filled with the members of our team for the first time.

"Wow, Payal! You employ all these people?" my mom asked, genuinely surprised, taking in everything.

"Yes," I replied.

At that point, I had been working on ClassPass for five years, and my mother's reaction made me think about all that we had been through as a team. It was so easy for me to get caught up in celebrating the members and partners we worked with, but in that moment, I also realized how meaningful it was sharing this journey with the people who had built this with me. People who had left their secure jobs to take a bet on this product and vision. People who started in customer service and went on to open new markets and get promoted to leadership positions. People who began working at ClassPass when they were single, and then fell in love and got married and had kids. All our lives had changed so much. I realized that traveling this journey together was what was most rewarding—and it made me the most proud. Hours before our new office would be filled with everyone's energy, I thought about everything that had led here. I felt wonder and gratitude for the people who had placed their trust in me—and I appreciated that I never could have done any of this alone.

TEAM LIFE

From a young age, the knowledge and trust that I could rely on others unleashed me to dream. Performing at events throughout our community was a lot of responsibility for a child, but my parents always helped me make sure I had the right outfit and music prepared, and that I got to the event on time and was ready to go. My dad always found a way to drive me to dance practice, pick me up from cheerleading, and fix the stereos I constantly overplayed until they broke. My mom stayed up late to alter and iron the new chaniya cholis that were sent to me from India so they would look perfect when I performed.

My parents recognized how important dancing was to me, and they were willing to do whatever it took to help me make it happen. This showed me that if I took action to pursue what I loved and worked hard for, people would be willing to step up and support me. Whenever I had an idea, I never doubted my ability to get it done—not because I believed I could do it all myself, but because I knew I could find people to help me on my journey. This allowed me to think bigger than I would have otherwise.

Sa's weekend-long Premiere NYC Showcase was the culmination of a team effort. My sister, Avani, and brother-in-law, Arjun, served as event planners extraordinaire, making sure all the vendors and volunteers were on time. They also coordinated the front-office ticket sales so the audience could enter without a hitch. My mom dressed the dancers in complete synchronization, my dad drove us to the theater, and Usha Aunty served as my eyes and ears so I could focus on performing. A music industry friend gave me feedback on the music and optimized it for the theater's speakers. One of the dancers was a graphic designer, and she helped create the program and make the costumes. Other friends and family members volunteered to help sign in and usher guests. These people were a part of my personal team, which enhanced my strengths, filled in for my weaknesses, and did whatever it took to help the show succeed.

This is what I call Team Life, the phenomenon of having a few people close to us who support us and are invested in our success. I am lucky to have a family that is supportive. Not everyone has that. Team Life is about building our own circle of support from family, friends, teachers, mentors, colleagues, and bosses who can help support us as we follow our calling.

DESIGN YOUR TEAM

Throughout life, but especially when pursuing your calling, you want a team that can help you keep pushing forward through obstacles and setbacks. When I had the opportunity to put together teams for Sa and ClassPass, I thought long and hard about what types of people I worked best with, and I was intentional about recruiting based on these characteristics. Some personality types simply work better together than others and allow both people in the relationship to support and give to each other.

When I started Sa, I didn't simply look for the best dancers. I thought about what would make a Sa dancer unique and what characteristics would help us work together as a cohesive whole. I came up with three pillars: technique, expression, and respect. These were the most important traits a Sa dancer could possess. With this in mind, it was much easier to recruit and select dancers, since I had concrete criteria. If someone was a fantastic dancer but didn't have strong emotional expressions, or if she didn't display respect to the rest of the group by showing up on time and giving her all, I knew she wouldn't be the right fit for us.

With ClassPass, I assessed what sort of team we needed for the company to succeed and who would be the best employees for me to lead. By then, I knew that I worked best with generally positive people who had an optimistic outlook, and who were humble and wanted to grow and learn. I also valued those who made good use of their most precious asset, time! The company pillars I created when making hiring decisions were: positivity, growth, and efficiency.

Establishing these pillars helped the company and me in many ways. As a leader, I knew I had to exude these values, and they gave employees a clear sense of what was expected of them and what they were meant to strive for. Before performance reviews, employees evaluated themselves based on these pillars, and we gave awards every year to the employees who most strongly exhibited these traits. I was able to thrive when surrounded by people at work, at Sa, and in my personal life who shared my foundational values and fit together seamlessly as a team. I also learned from experience that whenever we hired someone who didn't display these values, that hire tended to not work out.

Take a moment to consider who you might recruit for your own Team Life and what pillars you'd define (the Self-Check on page 123 helps address this). Are there certain types of people missing from your inner circle or energies that are absent from your life? Are there particular people you work well with? Pay attention to how people make you feel—and let this guide you when making decisions about who to bring into your life to help you reach your goals.

Ultimately, I suggest identifying a core team of three to five people who can help you move forward on your mission. Choose each person intentionally. Don't necessarily pick people because they are the most convenient or familiar. Not everyone we know will make an ideal team member for us, even when people care for us and are willing to help.

Having the right team is essential to living up to our potential. Gathering the right people is the engine that helps us accelerate. Consider the people you know: Who makes you want to be more and do more? Who leaves you feeling inspired or empowered? Of those who inspire you, do they also actively encourage you, offer helpful feedback and support, and ask questions that help you make good decisions? These are signs that someone is invested in your success and will be a good member of your team.

Sometimes, key people arrive unexpectedly. I met my good friend and eventual roommate Melanie at a Bollywood dance class in Manhattan. We quickly connected over our consulting jobs, but more importantly over our passions. She was determined and disciplined just like me, and we both were pursuing our side hustles, me dancing and Melanie acting. On Friday and Saturday nights, instead of going out, we shared our crafts with one another. Melanie practiced lines for her auditions, and I showed her the choreography I was working on. I often think back to how important that was, to have a friend and roommate like Melanie who encouraged my life path. A saying goes, "Great minds discuss ideas, average minds discuss events, small minds discuss people." To this day, Melanie and I share ideas, dream together, and talk about our ambitious goals whenever we meet. She was and remains part of my Team Life.

WHO DO YOU WORK WITH BEST?

We all work better with certain personality types than others, but do you know your own tendencies, preferences, and patterns? To explore this, consider any group project that went well, whether it was at work, at school, or in your personal life. Ask yourself the following questions:

1 How did you operate within the team? What role did you naturally gravitate toward?

2 What teammates did you work particularly well with and why?

3 What characteristics did they share that helped you work effectively?

Look for overlap in your answers, and then use this information to create three to four pillars. Then use these to evaluate who might be a good member of your personal or professional team. This way, whenever you meet someone new, you'll know whether or not they belong on your Team Life.

SEEK MENTORS AND TEACHERS

When pursuing your passion and building your Team Life, pay particular attention to identifying mentors and teachers who can guide you and push you. These are people who know the road you want to travel, either through training or life experience, and who are willing to impart their knowledge and invest in your success.

Keep in mind that a mentor relationship is different than a teacher or coach relationship. Teachers often possess the knowledge we need, and coaches can help us practice and train for a specific goal. We tend to seek out teachers and coaches when we have a particular challenge or skill to learn, and the relationship might end when we achieve or learn what we want. A mentor, on the other hand, is often a long-term relationship. They take an interest in our whole selves. Their focus isn't to help us succeed in one goal, but in everything we might attempt. Mentorships don't happen overnight. They often need cultivation and might develop slowly, but when a person is right for you, you both will feel a natural momentum and affinity.

I was lucky to find one of my mentors as a child, Usha Aunty, who exemplifies for me what a mentor is. I consider her family, though we aren't related. While she started as only my dance teacher, she has taught and guided me my entire life.

A few years back, Sa Dance Company was asked to perform at Lincoln Center for "Midsummer Night Swing." Usha Aunty is always the person I love to speak with when I'm laying out my vision. I told her that the organizers said we had as much as seven minutes to perform. "How long do you think the dance should be?" I asked. Without hesitation, she replied, "Seven minutes. Take every minute they give you to make an impact and show your culture." These are the types of lessons I always learn from Usha Aunty—she shows me how to never waste an opportunity and how to make the best of it.

Even though I don't see Usha Aunty as much these days, the relationship we have cultivated over thirty-five years is still one of the most profound in my life. She still coaches me on living to the fullest. I recently sent her a video of myself dancing, and she replied, "I would rather give you good advice than just praise you." She went on to comment about improving my footwork and seeking inspiration by studying videos of other incredible dancers and gurus. This is exactly what you want in a mentor—someone who will push you in new directions and encourage you to be your best, even when it's uncomfortable. Discomfort is often what keeps us from taking action toward our dreams, and sometimes we need other people to remind us of that. Support doesn't mean blind enthusiasm. It means honesty and constructive feedback. Thanks to Usha Aunty, I welcome challenges and know how to work through them, and that, more than almost anything, has helped me achieve my goals. When I feel scared or intimidated now, I think to myself, "I've been here before." I'm familiar with being in a room with someone who's pushing me. In fact, I seek it out because I know it makes me better.

Other important teachers have appeared in my life who have played different roles. After Sanjiv and I were attacked in a coffee shop, I struggled with feelings of victimization. I felt weak and helpless, and I knew I needed to build myself up, emotionally and physically. Up until that point, I had rarely exercised outside of dance. I don't think I even knew what a plank was! This gave me a good incentive to use ClassPass for myself. I began booking and experimenting with a range of different fitness classes.

After trying a few, I found an instructor named Patricia who taught me to lift weights in a way that felt right for my body type and fitness level. Patricia became a gateway into my personal fitness journey. With the confidence she helped me build, I explored other classes and methods, from barre to TRX and spin. A year later, I went back and thanked Patricia for helping me feel stronger and more powerful than I ever had before.

When we are younger, we have the benefit of many teachers and coaches to guide us. As we get older, as we get caught up in work and careers, this kind of relationship can become less common. Personally, this reiterated for me the importance of ClassPass, since it helps adults find these types of teacher and coach relationships during all phases of life. We all need that extra push and support at times, whether physically, mentally, or emotionally.

When I was starting ClassPass, I looked to others who had been there before me for guidance. I initially thought of what we were building as an "OpenTable for classes," and I desperately wanted to meet someone who had done something similar. Cyrus Massoumi was then scaling Zocdoc, a reservation and ratings system for doctors, and he also lived in New York. I asked everyone I knew to help me meet him. Eventually, he heard about me from three or four individuals (yup, that's hustle!), which piqued his interest and spurred him to reply and offer to meet with me.

The meeting went well, but Cyrus said he didn't have time to officially advise me, and he wanted to learn more about me and the business before investing his time. I was a bit bummed, but a mentor relationship isn't made in one meeting. It takes care and attention on the part of both people; it has to develop naturally over time. Each person needs to feel they are providing and receiving value, and establishing that sometimes means staying in touch, communicating efficiently, and doing good work. That's why I continued to send follow-up emails to Cyrus updating him on the company's progress even though he wasn't formally involved. Eight months later I told him about how we pivoted. "You might be onto something," he responded, and he told me that the Zocdoc employees were all using our Passport product.

At that point, after watching my progress firsthand, he said that he'd be happy to serve as an advisor to me and the company. Developing a mentor, especially in business, is not only about getting in the door; it's about staying on someone's radar. All meaningful relationships are built by investing in them over time.

Always remember, it's the work you do plus the people you work with that will determine how far you go.

CULTIVATE YOUR TEAM LIFE

The idea of networking has always made me a little uneasy. I consider myself a "mission-oriented extrovert." When I'm talking about my mission, I am naturally outgoing and talkative. But I'm not always so good at small talk. That's why I have intentionally surrounded myself with people who have a natural ease in these situations.

Sanjiv is one of those people. He can talk to anyone. When we were starting out, we didn't know anyone in the tech world in New York City, so we invested in tickets to a big conference with the intention of meeting people. These tickets were way more costly than we could afford, but we knew that with all the important industry players in attendance, we would be one person away from everyone we needed to meet to help get ClassPass to the next level. That made it a worthy investment, and we selected our sessions carefully. On the first day of the conference, I came out of a thirty-minute session to find Sanjiv surrounded by a group of ten people—all laughing about something he had said.

This continued as the conference went on and we ended up meeting almost every person there. We left that conference with a stack of business cards, meetings lined up for the next week with potential advisors, invitations to parties, and an introduction to another get-together of tech entrepreneurs. A few of these people ended up becoming some of my most important investors in and advisors to ClassPass and even close friends, all from the momentum of attending one conference.

The relationships I have built have been such an important force in propelling my success and my abilities as a leader, and beyond that, how to stay true to myself and my calling. To begin building your community, consider tapping into an existing group of people who are going through something similar, whatever matches your goals and purpose. Social media makes this easy. Search out Facebook groups, reach out to inspiring people on Instagram, attend an event or conference, or sign up for a class that might attract like-minded people. Online conferences have erased geographical limits. There are events online for nearly every industry. Find out where the people you want to connect with are—and get to know them.

As you do this, keep an eye out for potential mentors. Ask for introductions from people at work and through your network of friends and family. You may be surprised by how many people are eager to step up and help you. Introductions are a valuable currency, so even if your friends are connected to high-profile people, you must earn that connection. People ask me all the time to introduce them to people I know, but I respect those relationships too much to introduce anyone who hasn't proven themselves worthy of their time. Always be mindful about how you make any request for an introduction. The way you communicate is correlated to the response you'll receive. Make emails easily forwardable if you are asking for an introduction. Be very clear about what you are asking and make sure your request is easy to execute. If requests take too much time, people are less inclined to do it.

One of the most critical introductions was when I met Fritz. I was contemplating raising a large round of funding from larger VC firms, and David Tisch, who had been a tremendous supporter of me since Techstars, told me to meet with a few angel investors first. I walked into Soho House in NYC and sat down with Fritz, ready to pull out my slides and go into my investor presentation, or "performance." But Fritz stopped me and said, "Wait, just tell me what you're building and why. We don't need slides." I was a bit thrown off, but I went back to my passion for storytelling, explaining my background and the idea and vision for ClassPass. I left the meeting feeling like I was on fire. When I got back to my desk that afternoon, an email from Fritz was waiting. "Payal, I'd love to help you build this. I think you may be building the next Uber." Fritz became a central part of my core team from that day forward.

Remember, it doesn't matter if you are meeting people at the top of your industry or superstars in the field. What's most important is finding people you truly connect with. The best mentors and teachers care about you; that's their real value. Further, if you present yourself authentically, share what you truly want and need, and perhaps most importantly, prove yourself through passion, drive, and hard work, you will find people who will want to help you. One introduction will lead to another, which will lead to another, and if you establish a strong reputation, this will precede you and unlock more doors.

At Warner, I was working on the business side, and every so often we had meetings with the artist management team, where I met one of the senior leaders, Roger Gold. I followed up with Roger after one of those meetings to learn more about what he did, and he became a mentor. We would meet for lunch, and he taught me about his role and career and took an interest in mine, offering an ear to listen and advise. He was the one who introduced me to Anjula Acharia, who invested in and became an advisor to ClassPass after I stayed up all night to revise my business plan. If I had never developed a mentor relationship with Roger, I might never have met her!

Anjula and I have also developed a strong and enduring mentor relationship. Sometimes Anjula and I connect every day, and other times we go for months without chatting. The important thing is that when we do talk, we are both totally present, and it's clear that she's invested in my success over the long term. When ClassPass was going through iterations and facing roadblocks, she told me, "You're an album, not a single," a line she borrowed from one of her mentors, record mogul Jimmy Iovine. I know she will always be there for me because she cares about the big picture of my life and career.

As all this happens, consider two more things. First, just as people are paving the road for you, think about how you can pave the road for others. How can you lessen the slope for someone who shares your passion and might follow your lead? Give back by sharing your own best advice and helping to ease the climb for someone else to reach their potential. Personally, I'm cognizant of the impact of my identity on others, whether other female founders or Indian women trying to chart their own path. I hope my journey will make it easier for people like me to succeed. One of the best parts is that many of the people I have mentored have become great inspirations to me and are now a part of my own Team Life.

Second, consider how you can give back to those who are investing their time and energy in helping you. Reach out with notes of appreciation for all the ways people give you the strength, inspiration, knowledge, and resources to fly. Do this with the people who are currently helping you, and even better, express gratitude to those who have helped you get this far.

If someone has touched your life, tell them! People don't always know when they've been helpful. Take a moment to reach out and show your gratitude. This will likely motivate the other person to invest even more in you and then go and help someone else.

MAKE AN AUTHENTIC, MEMORABLE IMPRESSION

SELF-CHECK POINT

Networking can feel phony, but sharing your authentic self can be all the difference in the impressions you make. For this exercise, imagine you are at a networking event with influential people in your industry. You find yourself in the middle of a group of strangers and someone asks you to introduce yourself. Outside of your title and where you work, what else do you say? To generate some stories, ask yourself the following questions:

1   What are three words the people who know you best
    would use to describe you? (These don't have to be
    work related.)

2   Was there a time that you demonstrated each of
    those traits?

3   What's a unique thing about you?

With this material in your back pocket, you can enter any
situation feeling confident that you can introduce yourself in
an effective way that lets people see the real you. People may
not remember your title, but they will remember your energy
and your unique stories.

CHANCE ENCOUNTERS

In 2009, a few weeks after the Sa Dance Company was featured
in the *New York Times*, we performed at a gala event that was
attended by Mira Nair, the internationally acclaimed director of
Monsoon Wedding and many other films. After the performance,
an assistant approached and said that Mira wanted to meet me.
I was so excited, and when Mira told me how much she loved
our performance and asked for my email address, I felt like I was
dying inside—in a good way!

The next morning, I had an email from Mira. The subject line
read, "Your exquisite work," and she asked Sa to perform at her
upcoming Diwali party. That party was an amazing experience
that helped create a sense of momentum for Sa. A year later, I
asked Mira to speak at Sa's weekend-long showcase as our guest
of honor. Her acceptance helped give Sa the credibility it needed,
and Mira's supportive words also left an impact on all those who
attended our showcase.

This moment made me realize that if we put our passion out there, opportunities and, more importantly, the right people can come our way. Over the last decade, I've continued to build a wonderful relationship with Mira, choreographing dances for her personally as well as helping to promote and workshop the Broadway rendition of her movie *Monsoon Wedding*. Her support has been a huge influence on my creative work as well as my business pursuits. All from one chance encounter!

A similar thing happened in the early days of ClassPass. When I first started ClassPass, a company called Mindbody served as the backend software most studios used to run their businesses and process reservations. Like many other companies, we were able to use their technology to help build ClassPass. Mindbody was founded by Rick Stollmeyer with a vision to connect the world to wellness. His wife, Jill, who also worked at the company, saw Sanjiv and me on the cover of *Inc.* magazine and encouraged him to meet with us. They came to New York and we had dinner. "One day we will work closely together," Rick said. Four years later I bumped into him at a big industry conference, where he invited me onstage to share my company with all the fitness giants in the room. Over this last decade, our partnership continued to strengthen and grow, ultimately inspiring us to join forces as one company. What started as a casual dinner meet and greet led to one of the most important milestones in the journey of ClassPass and for me as an entrepreneur.

We don't always know how the people we meet can change our story and impact our life. From teamwork and partnerships to recommendations and inspiration, we are all connected. Remember, it was my chance encounter of meeting my friend Parul's entrepreneur friends in San Francisco that opened my eyes to the possibility of even becoming an entrepreneur myself. People are a huge part of making our dreams come true, so we should treat every meeting and opportunity as if it might be the one that changes our life.

Who I surround myself with is my decision.

8

TIME

How are you investing your most valuable asset?

BEFORE I GAVE BIRTH AND BECAME a mom, I never understood what motherhood truly entailed. Most importantly, how it was really a 24/7 job! I have always been thoughtful about my time and good at delegating, but this bundle of joy added a new complexity. My dreams competed for time with my baby and vice versa. So I needed to prioritize and schedule in what was most important. While I was used to being able to dedicate whatever time I wanted to work, dance, socialize, and be in the zone, I needed to find a way to continue doing what I loved and also be the mom I wanted to be for my son, Zayn. I determined that meant quality time with my son instead of quantity. The way I instituted that was by planning meaningful, fully present blocked hours of time with my baby.

The mornings were a sacred time I could share with Zayn while the world felt a bit more quiet. The afternoons before bedtime were when Nick, Zayn, and I would go for walks and do activities together. I worked with Nick to define this schedule and plan childcare each week so I had the best of both my worlds. At times, it was hard to switch gears from boardroom to baby, but I found creating this plan allowed me to welcome this time and be less distracted. This process felt strikingly similar. There have been other times in my life that I had to manage my time to nurture my passions and ambition.

Ever since I was young, I've planned my schedule meticulously and used my hours well. What does that mean exactly? I am present and focused on whatever I am doing. I literally can read a book in the middle of a party if I have to. This has helped me do more with fewer hours. Though it seems counterintuitive, taking time to plan my time gives me more time. To create more productive hours in a day, I've found I don't have to go to bed later or wake up earlier. I simply need to use my time productively and purposefully.

Of all the constraints that can hold us back from reaching our potential, time seems fixed, unchangeable. Many believe it's something we have no control over and lament everything they can't do because they don't have enough time. We each have twenty-four hours in a day (as the popular saying goes, "The same number of hours as Beyoncé"), and it feels like that's never enough to meet our responsibilities, pursue our passions, take care of ourselves, and maybe even sleep—right?

Time is our most valuable asset, and it is the one people abuse the most. The truth is, we have complete ownership of our time, as well as of our entire life. Our time belongs to us. And this chapter shows you how to get the most out of those twenty-four hours each day by prioritizing, planning, and performing what matters to you.

SHOULD VERSUS MUST

I started ClassPass to help people utilize pockets of time to discover a new class or experience that can infuse more passion and joy into their lives. Now, I want to help you find those slices of time in your day that already exist and are being either wasted or overlooked. Of course, no matter how well we use our time, it won't be possible for every hour of the day to go toward what we enjoy. But to take control of our time, we need to identify what is most important. That means important to you and no one else. In other words, what are your priorities—the things you need to do and the ones you most want to find time for?

It's amazing how often we can go through our days on autopilot, and without thinking about how we want to use our time. Our days run us instead of us running them. It's easy to sit back and let work and family and social obligations take over, but this is not how to live a life of passion and purpose. To achieve our potential, we must know what our priorities are and proactively make time for them.

The first step is to delineate between the things you feel you "should" do out of guilt or obligation and the things you "must" do because they are your key responsibilities or are essential for achieving your goals and purpose. Let's start with your "musts." These include the necessary tasks of everyday life, like earning an income, caring for your family, paying your bills, and so on. These aren't always fun and exciting, but then again, not all of the tasks connected to our dreams will be fun and exciting, either. But if something is necessary to move you in the right direction, then it is a must and worth making sacrifices for.

Next, identify your "shoulds." These are things we do out of a sense of obligation or guilt, but they aren't truly necessary and don't serve our time and energy. Eliminating shoulds is how we maximize our time. Start by paying attention to moments when you find yourself thinking or even saying out loud that you "should" do something. Then ask why. Is it to please others or because you feel you must do something to live the life you want? If it's the former, consider removing this activity from your schedule and working with others to adjust what they expect of you.

Guilt often keeps us from focusing on our own priorities. This is especially true for women, who often feel pressured to nurture and put the goals of others first. Women can often end up living their lives for someone else because they feel guilty prioritizing their own dreams. My weapon against guilt is my sense of purpose and my priorities. When we have a calling, it's easy to say no to someone else's plan without feeling guilty. After all, when we feel strongly about the path that we're on, why would we say yes to anything that might take us off course?

Guilt is one of the biggest challenges we face when trying to protect our priorities. It takes practice to build the resilience to say no without guilt, but we should never feel guilty about having something amazing that we need to do in this world and making sacrifices to do it. I will be honest: This is not easy. It involves making hard choices, and it takes practice to distinguish genuine "musts" from "shoulds." Get real with yourself about how your current choices are making you feel. How often do you let guilt and a sense of obligation guide your choices and take up your time?

I've had to make hard choices with my time to build Class-Pass, continue to dance, and even write this book! I've missed weddings, birthdays, travel experiences, and more. Sometimes, activities that we truly enjoy qualify as "shoulds," and if we don't do them, we don't feel guilt so much as disappointment for ourselves, and even experience a bit of FOMO. However, time for our life goals and priorities has to come from somewhere, and protecting and finding time for our passions inherently means making trade-offs. The important thing is to do it on our own terms.

We take control of our time when we say no to shoulds without guilt in favor of a wholehearted yes to our musts.

Below, I provide techniques for planning your time as efficiently as possible and achieving those plans. Along the way, continue to ask yourself if each event, meeting, phone call, or coffee date is a should or a must. If it is a should, can you take back that time and use it for something that is more important to you right now? Make sure that the things that you say yes to serve your higher purpose. This is something you should never, ever feel guilty for.

HOW ARE YOU INVESTING YOUR MOST VALUABLE ASSET?

SELF-CHECK POINT

Take a few minutes to reflect on your past week either by jogging your memory of what you did each day or by looking at your past week's calendar in order to gain a better understanding of how you are currently investing your time, which is your most valuable asset. Answer these questions:

1   In the last week, what things did you do that you really wanted to do?

2   What did you do out of obligation, or a should? (Be honest!)

3   What things coming up are you most looking forward to? Anything you are dreading?

Remember, how you spend your time is a conscious choice, not something that happens randomly. You are not obligated to say yes to every invitation, respond to every text, or set up a meeting with someone just because they ask. Consider the events and activities you listed: Which could you have said no to as a way of saying yes to yourself?

THE ART OF SCHEDULING

Once you know what your priorities are (which is what part 3 focuses on), the second step is to create a plan to make them happen. This comes down to scheduling. I've been a scheduling maniac ever since I was a young girl. Every day was like a race with myself to get everything done—cheerleading practice, homework, dinner with my family, more homework, dance practice, in bed by ten. But instead of finding it stressful, it was motivating. Scheduling the things that I had to do gave me the freedom to do the things I wanted to do. I never thought, *Oh, no, I only have two hours to do all of my homework.* Instead, I saw it as a fun challenge. I asked myself, *How can I get all of this done in two hours?* Over the years, I've mastered the skill of scheduling to get the most out of my life, and this has helped me take control of my time instead of allowing it to limit me.

The scheduling practice I recommend is the one I still use. This thirty-minute session saves me countless hours each week, not to mention it earns me a clear head when I sleep at night. Every Sunday night (and I recommend doing this once a week), I settle into the coziest chair in the living room, pull out my laptop, and open my "Payal Weekly Priorities" document. This is based on my bigger, long-term goals (which are also addressed in part 3). These items can range from appointments I need to schedule to important meetings or work sessions I need to have to dance pieces I need to work on, and even plans I want to make with friends or family members. Next, I estimate how long it will take to complete each item on my list. Then, I click on my calendar for the upcoming week and compare what's on there with everything I've just written down. How well is my schedule aligned with my priorities?

Some weeks, there's already a lot of overlap between my schedule and my priorities. Other times, there is enough white space for me to fill in time blocks to complete the tasks on my list. It's like completing a puzzle, searching for the perfect block of time in which to fit the right task. Other weeks, I look at my calendar and see that it's already packed with meetings and other obligations that don't reflect the priorities I've written down. When this happens, I go through each commitment and decide whether to keep it, cancel it, or reschedule it to make time for what is more important to me at that moment. Further, I don't feel bad canceling or rescheduling because I know how ineffective I'll be if I spread myself too thin, which is a lose-lose when it comes to my priorities.

This is why I write down my list of priorities *first*, before glancing at my calendar to see what's already on there. If I started by looking at the calendar and found it full, I might be tempted to just leave it as is. No need to come up with a new list of things to do—I'm already busy enough! Aren't we all?! Starting with my list of priorities is my way of holding myself accountable. If these are the things that are most important to me, then I need to plan to spend most of my week focused on them. These are my musts.

The great news is that each week, and each day, presents a new opportunity. I plan my time so I can make the most of it, but I build in some flexibility, since nothing ever flows exactly as planned. Here is what this looks like. Back when ClassPass started taking off, we were launching in a new city every few weeks and hiring across the organization, and I was planning Sa's second weekend-long NYC Showcase. It was an incredible amount to accomplish in a short period of time. But I wasn't overwhelmed because my approach to scheduling ensured I had time for it all.

Every morning, I got up early and went for a twenty-minute run to help wake up my mind and body. I also used this time to work through problems in my head and meditate on the day ahead. Then I showered and got to the office by 9 a.m. I didn't schedule meetings until 10 a.m., so I could use that hour to go through my emails. From 10 a.m. until the afternoon, I was in back-to-back meetings. Even then I tried to be as efficient as possible with my back-to-back meeting hack. For example, I didn't automatically schedule meetings for an hour or even half an hour. Instead, I looked at every meeting request and thought about how much time it would need. If it was a quick check-in with a team member or a new-hire meeting, I blocked fifteen minutes. This freed up multiple pockets of time throughout my day to check other small tasks off my list.

In the late afternoon, I tried to leave the office to attend a class and open my mind again for more creative work in the evening. Oftentimes, people try to power through hour after hour of work, but if we're sitting at our desk for seven hours straight, we're wasting some of that time. By taking a break from work to attend a class, I gained something out of that time and returned to work reenergized and rejuvenated. I've always encouraged my team at ClassPass to do the same thing. I love it when someone tells me that they need to duck out of a meeting to go to class because I know they'll come back to work refreshed and ready to crush the rest of the day.

For important priorities that can sometimes be flexible, like working out, I seek out multiple classes or workouts in a day in case something comes up that prevents me from attending my first choice. I think of this as having a backup workout plan for my day. This is like planned spontaneity, which ensures I do what's important to me each day. Some tasks, especially creative ones, take longer than expected. I never want to have to stop myself in the middle of a flow because it's time to go to class. The point is to be liberated by my schedule, not constrained by it.

I used the early evening hours for brainstorming, and then tackled more emails from 6 to 7 p.m. while eating dinner at my desk. Then I changed and went to dance practice from 8 to 10 p.m. This, too, opened my mind to creative thinking, and I often spent the last few hours of the night on strategic planning for the company. My weekends were also scheduled tightly, but with more time for choreography or longer strategy meetings, since I didn't have emails and meetings tugging at my mind.

Since getting married and becoming a parent, my Sunday-night scheduling ritual has grown even more important. Time management isn't about creating a busy calendar or filling every spare minute with our goals; it's about respecting our time and priorities. I want to maximize time with my little one but still fit in all my ambitious goals. The only way to do that is through planning.

GETTING THE HIGHEST RETURN ON INVESTMENT

While we are the only ones who can schedule our time, we also can't do everything ourselves. We don't have enough time, and if we try, we often undermine our effectiveness and our most important priorities suffer. So even among all the items on our "must" list, we need to prioritize, and when we can, we should delegate those less-important priorities to others.

For instance, I once decided it was time to organize my home, but the idea of spending my entire weekend and more going through every drawer trying to clear out clutter, à la Marie Kondo, didn't feel like the best use of my time or my strength! I had other priorities that were more important, ones only I could do. While I knew there was another way to organize my home—hire someone else—I was reluctant to do that.

Growing up, my parents never hired someone to clean the house or help with personal or home-related tasks. The entire concept of delegating such jobs was foreign to me, and to be honest, it felt a bit embarrassing and taboo. Many people, women in particular, feel a social pressure or burden to do everything, and asking for help can feel like an expression of failure or inadequacy.

I've always liked this quote by businessman and bestselling author Harvey Mackay: "Time is free, but it is priceless. You can't own it, but you can use it. You can't keep it, but you can spend it. Once you've lost it, you can never get it back." Instead of wasting time feeling guilty about asking for help, I tried to look at the situation more objectively. I knew my hours were valuable, and the best way to spend them, the one with the highest return on investment, was running my company. Tasks like organizing my home might be important, but they weren't going to pay dividends in the long run.

So I hired someone, and then I started outsourcing other personal tasks, as many as I could. I was surprised to find that the more comfortable I grew delegating personal tasks, the more effective I became as a leader. I realized how much quicker and better someone who is an expert at something can be! Founders can tend to be controlling. The company is their baby, and in the beginning, they need to make each decision and watch every step. But as the company grows, if they don't let go of the urge to do and oversee everything themselves, it will hold back the company's growth and potential. The same is true in everyday life no matter what our life goals are. We need to create a support team and then trust them to execute. Over the years, I've become much more comfortable handing things off that aren't my strengths. I've learned other people can do certain things faster, and even better than me, which allows me to focus on what I am good at, which is a win for everyone.

In your own life, consider the tasks that need to get done but which you might delegate to others. These might be necessary household chores or certain aspects of your job that bring you no joy. One example is often the administrative demands of running a business or creative project; these can be ideal things to outsource, since that allows you to focus on the things you are passionate about. This doesn't necessarily mean hiring people and spending money. Consider your Team Life—your family, friends, and others—and who can help take on additional tasks.

Deciding when and what to delegate to others is part of figuring out what your time is worth. When you make decisions about how to schedule your time, ask yourself: *Is this task adding value to my life, my career, or my purpose?* If so, consider whether you need to be the one to do it, or if it just needs to get done. Prioritizing your time so that you focus first on the tasks only you can do provides the best return on your investment. For everything else, it may be worth outsourcing or delegating that task to someone else.

To evaluate this, first make a list of the tasks that you would like to delegate. Then, go through them one by one and write down roughly how much time this task takes to complete (in hours, days, or weeks), and figure out approximately how much it would cost to hire someone to do it for you. For example, estimate how much time it typically takes you to clean your house or apartment, and then get estimates from several cleaners about what they would charge.

Then, decide: What makes a better investment, your money or your time? If you didn't do this task, what would you use those hours for instead? If you saved that money, what would you use it for instead? Only you can decide what that investment of time or money is worth to *you.*

Finally, whenever you delegate or outsource a task, make sure to plan well and set clear expectations. Someone new typically requires more oversight or guidance at first, which of course takes more time. But this is an investment in the future and makes sure the person completes the task the way you want and as efficiently as possible. Every task has a cost in both time and money, but if you spend both wisely, they can often pay off exponentially.

OPTIMIZE YOUR PERFORMANCE

Just as everyone has their own unique patterns of success, everyone has their own daily rhythm, or the best ways they like to use their time. To the extent you can, schedule your own time with those preferences and patterns in mind, which will be more efficient and increase the return on your time investment. For instance, some people wake up fresh in the morning and ready to dive into complicated tasks. Others are most creative at night. Some people like to work uninterrupted for long stretches, while others do better by shifting tasks regularly. What works best might depend on what you're doing. While writing this book, I periodically interrupted long writing sessions with thirty-minute breaks to work on some choreography or dance. Dance worked a different part of my brain and helped me come back to my desk refreshed.

One thing I know about myself is that I'm terrible at doing multiple things at once, so it's important for me not to overlap too much. Because of this, I search for pockets of uninterrupted time. I love working on the plane so I can focus, while my husband can simultaneously rotate between emails, eating, and in-flight movies. We are all different. Either way, it's important to know yourself so you can schedule things to get the most out of your time.

One trade-off I don't recommend making is with sleep. Many people are tempted to sacrifice sleep to gain more time. But if we're tired from lack of sleep, we're less effective, and we can't operate at 100 percent of our capacity. When we are operating at full capacity, it's amazing how much we can get done in a short amount of time. How much sleep do you need to operate at your best? Don't skimp on that. I know that if I don't get seven to eight hours of sleep a night, then I can't function at full capacity. I'd rather take an extra thirty minutes to sleep than operate at 50 percent the entire day.

We all have the same number of hours in a day, but how we use our time has a tremendous impact on how much we can accomplish and how much fulfillment we can squeeze out of those hours. If your calendar is not serving you, then change it.

Do you find yourself exhausted at the end of every day? Then schedule time to rest during the day or get more sleep at night. Are you always late to meetings? Schedule a ten-minute buffer. Do you skip lunch? Schedule time to eat. Do you frequently rush your preparation before meetings? Schedule more prep time. Do you wish there was someone else who could do the cleaning, shopping, cooking, and yard work because you have better stuff to do? Assign chores to others in your household or hire someone! Make the changes that will make the best use of your most valuable asset.

MAKE THE MOST OF YOUR TIME | SELF-CHECK POINT

Raising awareness of our productivity patterns is the first step to shifting our schedules to make the most of our time. Be diligent, plan ahead, take ownership of your time, and you will gain the freedom for the things that matter most to you. Take a moment to reflect on how you feel at different points of the day. Ask yourself the following questions:

1   When is your mind the most alive? Can you block time for independent thinking and work during these hours?

2   When do you feel the most outgoing and engaged? Can you schedule most of your meetings for this time of day?

3   At what point in the day do you typically start to feel sluggish? Can you schedule a workout class or go for a quick run or walk during this time?

Make as many of these changes to your schedule as you can. Try them out for a week and track your productivity. Continue tweaking your schedule until your day fits your wants and needs. Life is ever-changing, so change with it.

PRESENCE OF MIND

Focus might be the most important skill for using our time efficiently. Developing presence of mind in the moment helps us get the most out of everything we do. Of course, this isn't always easy. Even when I schedule my time as efficiently as possible, I can find myself thinking about who to hire while in the middle of a team meeting, or unable to sleep at night because I'm planning a brand campaign.

When we think about how to squeeze more out of the limited number of hours in a day, we often fail to account for how many of those hours we lose to mental distractions or inefficient multitasking. Half focusing is the worst of both worlds. We don't actually complete any of the things we're working on, plus we feel stressed because our mind is constantly being pulled in a million directions. That's a perfect formula for losing sleep.

The same thing happens when we bounce back and forth between tasks or stop what we're doing to scroll social media. These interruptions can undermine our efficiency, especially when we are tackling complex problems that require our complete focus. When we get distracted or move on to something else and then go back to the task later, we have to reorient all over again and sometimes start from scratch.

My solution, which won't surprise you, is to schedule time for brainstorming and meeting preparation. I plan time ahead to work through solutions, to clarify intentions, to strategize company actions, and even to contemplate personal things I need to address.

In the past, when I found myself wrestling with a problem, my instinct was to drop everything and address it right then. But this wasn't always the most convenient time or productive approach. Now, I add decision-making to my to-do list, the same way I schedule a call or meeting. Once it's in my calendar, I know it will get done. I also know the reverse is true. If something is not on my calendar, I'll probably never get to it.

Taking time to schedule saves time in the long run, but more importantly, it makes the most of our time. The goal isn't to do everything quickly, but to be able to complete each task well.

Decision-making takes time; sometimes it takes research and consulting with others. It's a worthy investment!

If you find yourself getting distracted, try making a note of what's distracting you or even putting time in your calendar to get back to it later. Knowing that you will have a chance to think problems through fully at another time helps to refocus on the task at hand. Scheduling is also a good way to hold yourself accountable and cultivate the discipline to execute plans.

In addition, be aware of how you prefer to solve problems, and plan for that as well. Do you prefer to talk things through with a friend or mentor, to meditate, to journal, or to do something else? I like to talk issues through with someone I trust, someone who will ask me good questions. And if you want to talk to someone, don't just call; schedule a meeting or meal! Make sure you both come prepared and ready to solve the problem.

Yes, we all have only twenty-four hours in a day, but an hour isn't just an hour. An hour of focus and concentration can have the same output as an entire day of scattered thoughts and reactions. I'd rather work at my full capacity for one hour than work at half capacity for two hours. If I can focus and grind and get twice as much done in an hour, I gain an hour on the other end for something that recharges me—such as dance class, watching my favorite show with Nick, or even just time to dream!

CHOOSE YOUR TIME OVER ACHIEVEMENTS

In addition to scheduling and managing time on a daily basis, we also need to consider the big picture: Are we happy with our goals and our vision and what we are choosing to spend our time on? As Steve Jobs famously said, "Your time is limited, so don't waste it living someone else's life."

The growth of ClassPass brought tremendous change—for the company and for me. For one, Sanjiv had an idea for another company, so we discussed him leaving ClassPass to build a new start-up. Additionally, our team had grown substantially across three continents, and my role as CEO began to look very different from when I first founded the company. This is typical in most high-growth start-ups. I was still deeply invested in my mission, but my days were progressively becoming harder and harder.

While I tried to keep up with optimizing my time each day, I was consumed with day-to-day responsibilities that involved more "shoulds" than "musts." I didn't have time to think creatively. I didn't have the ability to focus on contributing to the company in the ways I found most meaningful. Instead,

I was busy trying to please investors, customers, partners, the media, and my team. And I was no longer dancing or connecting to my "why" behind all of this. I felt I was losing control of my time.

Nick and I were recently engaged, and we had just come back from a quick trip to the Caribbean. I remember needing to get away from work, a feeling I always tell people I hope they never have. I'd always loved what I did so much that the energy one might get from a vacation came from my work. I came home still feeling run-down and dreading going back to work the next day. I knew I needed to make a change for the benefit of my company and my own happiness.

I turned to Fritz as the person who could help. For years, he had been an amazing partner and a loyal and supportive member of my inner team; he was also chairman of the company's board of directors.

Luckily, Fritz soon became my right hand, and I started to feel better. I was able to invest my time and mind in what mattered. As time went on, I began to feel like the chairman position would be a better fit for me than the CEO role. I had started ClassPass to solve a problem in the world, not to have a big title.

But it was complicated. There was a lot of talk in the media about the importance of female CEOs, and I took my position as a role model for young girls and other women seriously. I didn't want any woman to look at my decision to no longer be CEO and feel that she didn't deserve to be a CEO. Furthermore, societal expectations are strong, and I felt pulled by this external call. What would people think if I gave up that role? Would they think I wasn't capable? Worse: Would they think I got fired? I began to wonder whether people would take me seriously without the

CEO title. Was I somehow less without this title—a title I never put any weight on?

Deep down, I knew that the worst thing I could do was hold on to a role that kept me busy with things I didn't want to be doing just because of what people would think. I had worked my way out of that constraint a long time ago! Furthermore, not living my life in pursuit of what I wanted to do would send young girls and anyone a wrong and inauthentic message. I had always succeeded when I went my own way. Could the solution be as simple as swapping titles with Fritz?

It turned out to be that simple. I felt like I could be a much better role model by spending my time in a way that allowed me to be my full, creative, authentic self. In giving up the CEO title, I gained much more—the ability to use my time meaningfully again and make contributions that mattered.

We are taught to value titles, but I found that the freedom over my time was what was most valuable—and what I had to protect.

Arriving at such big decisions is not something that you take lightly. By this point, I had adapted a method of setting goals and being acutely aware of what I wanted out of my life, both professionally and personally, which made making choices like this easier. This system—the LifePass Method—is what I will share in the final section of the book.

This method, which I will show you how to apply to your own life, has helped me continue to evolve and iterate as a leader, dancer, wife, mother, friend, and more. Outside of these roles, it's helped me progress in my mind, body, and soul. In moments of change, it has provided me with a constant, and in moments of confusion, it has given me the awareness I needed to focus and move toward what's important to me. I've never wanted to feel stagnant and the LifePass Method has helped me keep myself thriving and moving in all aspects of my life. I'm excited to see what it will do for you.

I am the only one in control of my time.

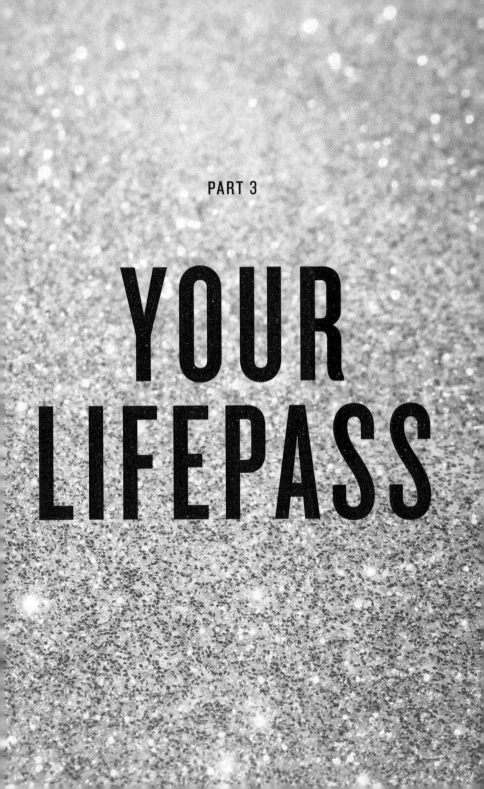

PART 3

YOUR
LIFEPASS

9

THE LIFEPASS METHOD

Reflect, dream, focus, and set goals!

TO GET CLASSPASS FROM AN IDEA in my head to a product that actually worked was something I poured all my time and energy into. Literally. And for years, I didn't realize that it came with a cost.

Then, over the 2013 holidays, I realized I was approaching New Year's all alone. It hit me—hard—that I had been so consumed with starting my company and getting it right that I had let everything else fade—my relationships, my home, my family, dance, and my health.

It had been my choice to go all-in on the company. ClassPass was my priority and deeply connected to my calling, and that had made saying no to everything else easy. For three years, I had been marching forward with single-minded focus, and I didn't regret it, but I started to recognize that maybe I had gone too far. The entrepreneurial journey can be lonely, and as one year was ending and another was beginning, I had to admit that I felt incredibly alone.

My last living grandparent, my dad's mother, had just passed away. My parents were in India for several months paying their respects. My sister, who always was thoughtful about including me in her plans, made her own arrangements to be with her in-laws, since I'd been MIA for so long. Everyone around me had taken time off work to enjoy other aspects of their lives. Me? I had very little going on in my life outside of work. I felt like I had been absent for so long everyone had forgotten about me. Although I was occasionally dating, I hadn't yet met Nick, and I felt there was little to no path to finding someone I wanted to spend my life with.

Since I had been single for so long, I was accustomed to being the third wheel, and I found a way to spend the holiday break tagging along with a friend and her parents on their vacation to the Caribbean. The time away was exactly what I needed. Without being so busy with work, I had space to see what was missing in my life. And I was motivated to make some changes. But how? On the flight home, with nothing to distract me, I focused on how to get my personal life on track. I needed to address the bigger picture for the sake of my health, my relationships, my happiness, and my company.

Throughout my life, whenever something wasn't working for me or things felt chaotic, I went back to my emotions and sense of fulfillment. I needed to tap into that feeling to gain strength and clarity and come up with a plan to move me in that direction. But I had only used this type of planning to set goals for my career and dance performances. Could I channel the same kind of energy and passion I had put toward those into the rest of my life?

It was time to approach my goals in a different way. During the last three roller-coaster years of iterating and building ClassPass, I learned to look forward instead of wallowing in the past. I knew that taking action, setting goals, and committing to a plan were the most important things I could do to change my current situation.

Right there on that plane, somewhere over the Atlantic Ocean, I started to develop a new goal-setting method to create fulfillment throughout my life based on how I wanted to *feel*, rather than solely on what I wanted to *accomplish*. This process put together all the lessons, tools, and tips I'd been developing throughout my career (and which I share in this book). Since then, this method has played a significant part in my life, and in this chapter, I share with you how to create and execute that method.

This step-by-step approach can help you identify your dreams; prioritize your time, money, and energy; and make progress toward specific, measurable goals across your life. I explain each step of the process so that you can apply this methodology to your own life. I also share my story of using this process to provide a real example and template. At the end of the chapter, you'll find other people's completed processes and reflections so you can see what it might look like— and the results. I hope that by using the LifePass Method, you too can change your life and accomplish more of what's meaningful to you.

GETTING STARTED

To get started, all you need is several blank pieces of paper and a pen. On the opposite page, you'll find a template you can follow along with. Over the next few pages, I'll take you through each step of the LifePass Method and each portion of the template. You're going to spend time doing each of the following: *Reflecting*, *Dreaming*, *Focusing*, and *Setting Goals*.

This process is rooted in you and your thoughts and wants. No one else's! So take this time for yourself to look inward and gain clarity for what you want to focus on next in all aspects of your life, big or small. Completing the entire method can take a couple hours if you do it all at once, which I recommend as the best approach. However, you can also tackle it over time if that is what works best with your schedule. As you go through each step, I'll share my own personal story and answers so you can see what the process looks like in action. At the end of this chapter, I share full examples of how other people interpreted the prompts and what goals and actions came out of their experience. But for now, let's focus on you. Spend time with the process because it's about to change your life.

Name

_____

Age, Title

REFLECT WORDS *(see p. 164 for examples)*

_____, _____, _____, _____, _____

DREAM WORDS *(see p. 168 for examples)*

_____, _____, _____, _____, _____

TIME ANALYSIS *(see p. 172 for examples and rank 1 to 10)*

_____ (#)	_____ (#)
_____ (#)	_____ (#)
_____ (#)	_____ (#)
_____ (#)	_____ (#)
_____ (#)	_____ (#)

GOALS

Focus Area 1

_____

_____

_____

Focus Area 2

_____

_____

_____

Focus Area 3

_____

_____

_____

Focus Area 4

_____

_____

_____

Focus Area 5

_____

_____

_____

REFLECT

How would you describe your past year?

Adventurous	Intelligent
Anxious	Intense
Charitable	Leadership
Community	Lonely
Confident	Lost
Connection	Love
Courageous	Passionate
Creative	Peaceful
Culture	Positive
Envious	Powerful
Exhausted	Purposeful
Family	Secure
Fear	Sharing
Focused	Spiritual
Friendship	Strong
Growth	Thankful
Happy	Transformative
Healthy	Travel
Hopeful	Uncertain
Independent	Wealth

Take five to ten minutes to think about where you were one year ago today. What was going on in your life? Situate yourself in the moment and how you felt. Once you have that in mind, think about the entire year that's transpired since then. What themes present themselves? What emotions and thoughts were most prevalent? What were the high points? The low points? Think about everything—work, personal life, health and fitness, relationships, and so on. Look back at your calendar or even revisit your journal (if you keep one) to remind yourself of what you were experiencing and how you were feeling.

Next, on a piece of scratch paper, write down a list of words that you feel characterize the past year. These can be emotions or themes, and most people will have a combination of positive and negative words, even in the best of years. Write down everything that comes to mind, and then choose the four to five words that together best describe the past year.

I've provided a list of sample words on the opposite page to kick-start your thinking, but this is not meant to be limiting. Write down any words that come to mind.

Once you have your list, review it to make sure it sums up your year. If you need to add or change words, do so.

> When you have a handful of words that you feel fully capture your emotions and experiences as you reflect on the year, write them across the top of a clean sheet of paper similar to the template provided. These are your reflect words.

Payal

REFLECT WORDS

Unpredictable, Lonely, Passionate, Focused, Unhealthy

DREAM WORDS

_____, _____, _____, _____, _____

TIME ANALYSIS

_____ (#)		_____ (#)	
_____ (#)		_____ (#)	
_____ (#)		_____ (#)	
_____ (#)		_____ (#)	
_____ (#)		_____ (#)	

GOALS

Focus Area 1

_____
_____
_____

Focus Area 2

_____
_____
_____

Focus Area 3

_____
_____
_____

Focus Area 4

_____
_____
_____

Focus Area 5

_____
_____
_____

Reflect: My Story

When I came up with this approach, I knew that before I could fix my personal life, I had to assess where I currently stood. In order to move forward, I had to know where I was starting. The past few years had been my most successful from a professional standpoint, but my personal life told another story. I could not continue down this path. The first thing I did was to reflect on the past year. I looked back at my calendar to remind myself of where I had gone, what I had done, and with whom I had spent time during my last trip around the sun.

Then, I closed my eyes and asked myself how everything I'd done over the last year had made me feel. What were the key questions that had come up again and again? Were there issues or conflicts with which I struggled, or emotions that permeated? Without censoring myself, I wrote down all the words, both positive and negative, that came to mind that summed up the year. Then I went over that list and pared them down to the five words that truly characterized it. They were *Unpredictable, Lonely, Passionate, Focused,* and *Unhealthy.*

DREAM

Where do you want to go?

Adventurous	Leadership
Charitable	Love
Community	Passionate
Confident	Peaceful
Connection	Positive
Courageous	Powerful
Creative	Purposeful
Culture	Secure
Family	Sharing
Focused	Spiritual
Friendship	Strong
Growth	Thankful
Healthy	Transformative
Hopeful	Travel
Intelligent	Wealth

Next, take five to ten minutes to pretend that you are doing this same evaluation a year from now. What do you hope will have happened? Really open your mind. Imagine that constraints don't exist. If they do, when it's time to set your goals, you can work through them using the tools in this book. Don't let yourself be held back by fear or someone else's definition of success. For now, imagine what happiness and success would be on your own terms, without worrying if it's realistic.

On a separate piece of scratch paper, write down a list of words that sums up the year you hope it will be. What would you like to be able to say? You might use the same words that you used to describe the previous year, or you might use entirely new words. Either is fine as long as you are honest with yourself about what you want the next year to embody. I've provided a list of sample words as inspiration on the opposite page, but don't let them limit you. Write down any words that come to mind.

> Once you have a list of words, whittle them down to four or five words that most speak to you. These are your dream words for the coming year. Write these down on the piece of paper under your reflect words.

As you set goals later in the process, these name the themes you will be aiming for. These words are important, so make sure the final list feels exciting and motivating. Before moving on, meditate on your dream words and anchor yourself in the mindset to move in that direction.

Payal

REFLECT WORDS

Unpredictable, Lonely, Passionate, Focused, Unhealthy

DREAM WORDS

Leadership, Strength, Growth, Stability, Performance (dance)

TIME ANALYSIS

_____ (#)		_____ (#)	
_____ (#)		_____ (#)	
_____ (#)		_____ (#)	
_____ (#)		_____ (#)	
_____ (#)		_____ (#)	

GOALS

Focus Area 1

_____
_____
_____

Focus Area 2

_____
_____
_____

Focus Area 3

_____
_____
_____

Focus Area 4

_____
_____
_____

Focus Area 5

_____
_____
_____

Dream: My Story

As my flight continued on, I began to think about how I was currently spending my time and what I wanted to change. I longed to dance more and perform again. Work had taken over my life, and I needed to make some hard decisions about leadership at ClassPass. I wasn't feeling physically strong—I could barely make it through one fitness class—and I had to regain control of my health. When it came to my personal life, it wasn't just that I wanted to get married. I wanted to feel loved and secure in a relationship that would stand the test of time.

I imagined myself a year from now, standing in my strength, performing again, living up to my potential as a leader so the company could continue to grow and thrive. I wrote down *Leadership, Strength, Growth, Stability,* and *Performance (dance).* Then I closed my eyes and repeated those words to myself silently, thinking about how everything I would do over the next year would be moving me powerfully in the direction of these themes.

FOCUS

What are your priorities?

Acting

Beauty

Caretaking

Cleaning

Cooking

Creation

Dining

Drinking

Education

Teaching

Travel

Entertainment

Exploring

Family

Fitness

Friends

Health

Kids

Leadership

Learning a skill

Lounging

Meditation

Partying

Personal time

Reading

Relationship

Shopping

Sleep

Social media

Training

Volunteering

Work

Writing

Next, we are going to track your time.

> Take five minutes, and under your dream words write down all the areas of your life that you currently spend any significant amount of time on. This is your time analysis.

It's important to be honest. Include everything that takes up to several hours of your day or week, from work, school, and family obligations to friend time, browsing social media, and sitting on the couch watching TV. Relaxation is okay! Also, this list will most likely include things that you want to spend less time on. In a way, that's the point. You want to track everything, including what you aren't enjoying, in order to free up time for your genuine priorities and the new things you want to do.

Look at the sample list on the opposite page for inspiration. If there are certain areas that take up a significant portion of your time, break it down into subtopics. For instance, don't just write down "work." Work typically consists of many activities depending on the field you are in. For example, it could break down into the subcategories of meetings, creative work, leading, and so on. While at work, what do you do that takes up the bulk of your time? List each area.

Likewise, break categories like "family" or "relationships" into subcategories. Separate time with your partner or kids from time spent with friends, and so on. Caring for elderly parents would be a different category than taking care of a new baby.

> Next, add areas that don't currently exist in your life but you want to add.

For instance, write down if you want to start going to the gym, traveling, earning a degree, or learning a new skill. While you can write down anything, be selective, and choose things that relate to your calling or that embody your dream words. Make sure to only add things that are important, and only things that are important to you and not others.

Rating Your Time Analysis

Now it's time to evaluate each area in terms of whether or not that specific part of your life is currently moving you in the direction of your dream words.

> Next to each area in your time analysis, give it a rating on a scale of 1 to 10.

A rating of 1 means this area of your life doesn't feel aligned at all with your dream words; a rating of 5 means it is somewhat aligned with your dream words; and a score of 10 indicates that this area is very aligned with your dream words.

A low score doesn't necessarily mean something to get rid of in your life. Instead, it indicates one of three things:

1. *This area is currently missing from your life, so it's rated low, but you want to increase it. Areas that I see commonly ignored include hobbies and passions as well as seeing important friends and self-care.*

2. *This area is not aligned with your dream words, but it is still important. It may reflect your responsibilities or*

values. One example is work. You may like your job but
not all of your responsibilities, some of which may not
be aligned with your purpose. Or your entire job may
not be aligned but you need the income. When it's time
to set goals, you can focus on infusing these areas with
passion and meaning.

3. *This area is not aligned with your dream words and it's*
   not important to you. When this is the case, it identifies
   an area to minimize or even cut from your life entirely.
   Whatever the reasons for spending time on this, this area
   is not serving you or moving you closer to your dream
   words. By minimizing or cutting these areas, you can free
   up time to invest in the activities you want to add.

Focus Areas to Work On

To create change, we need to focus on making time for that change to happen. The next step is choosing the areas you want to focus on and creating a plan for how to spend your time in those areas.

When it comes to planning, treat your dream words as your long-term goals for the year. They are not meant to change but to remain the same. On the other hand, your focus areas and the respective goals you will set as we continue on will cover the next three months only. Every quarter, you will review and revise these areas and goals as you move closer to your dream words.

You might be surprised by how much you can accomplish in three months. This period of time also helps eliminate unreasonable pressures and expectations to accomplish meaningful change in a day or a week. At the same time, a quarter of the year will pass by very quickly and give you an opportunity to recalibrate or change your goals as appropriate.

By hyper-focusing on your focus areas for a quarter at a time, you will have consistent opportunities to assess how things are going and make adjustments when you set your next round of goals. The point isn't to radically change your entire life from one quarter to the next, but to give yourself regular opportunities to tweak what you are doing and create pockets of time that you can use to inject passion into different areas of your life, while consistently moving toward your dream words.

This process keeps your goals and expectations manageable; every effort is finite. If something isn't working, you can shift in three months. This gives you permission to change focus and keeps you moving forward into the next moment in a positive way. It also can give you the confidence to try something new, knowing it's a short-term commitment. Most of all, it can give you a greater sense of control over your life. If something is absent from your life for a period of time, it's because you've decided that other things are more important at that moment. You are in charge of your own priorities.

To choose your focus areas for these next three months, go back to your rated time analysis and identify four to five areas that are important and that you are motivated to work on. Improvement can range from small changes to huge transformations. What matters is your excitement to do the work in them. This is an opportunity to decide which areas of your life need your attention right now. By setting tangible goals in these areas, the parts of your life that are currently the least fulfilling will begin to feel more defined by passion and purpose.

Circle these areas within your time analysis. These are your focus areas for the next three months.

With your priorities and dream words set, you are now ready to create an actionable plan.

Payal

REFLECT WORDS

Unpredictable, Lonely, Passionate, Focused, Unhealthy

DREAM WORDS

Leadership, Growth, Strength, Performance (dance), Stability

TIME ANALYSIS

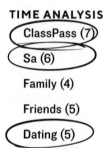

ClassPass (7)

Sa (6)

Family (4)

Friends (5)

Dating (5)

Working Out (7)

Travel (3)

Self-Care (4)

Health (3)

GOALS

Focus Area 1

_____

_____

_____

Focus Area 2

_____

_____

_____

Focus Area 3

_____

_____

_____

Focus Area 4

_____

_____

_____

Focus Area 5

_____

_____

_____

Prioritize: My Story

I wanted to manifest my dream words in all areas of my life, but I had to determine which areas of my life needed attention at that moment.

The big buckets in my life at the time were ClassPass, Sa, Family, Friends. Relationships, Working Out, and Travel. The ones I decided to include that were nonexistent were Self-Care and Health. After reflecting and rating myself in each area, I decided to focus on ClassPass, Sa, Relationships, Health, and Working Out.

This idea alone felt incredibly liberating. Instead of trying to be all things to all people all at once, or attempting to succeed at everything and feeling like I was failing at everything, I had a chance to decide how much time and attention to give to each different part of my life. I knew I would never find complete balance. Balance is not the objective. Instead, I wanted to gain momentum in the right direction, the direction of my choice. There is no such thing as work/life balance. There are only work/life choices. You can't have it all at all times. At different points in life and even within a day, some things must take greater priority than others.

In the years since I developed the LifePass Method, people have often asked me how I manage my company, my passion for dance, my relationship with my husband, my baby, my big extended family, and self-care. I tell them it's all about priorities. If something is important to me, I will get to it when the time is right to focus on it and then I will give it my all.

SET GOALS

What's your plan?

Organize a girls' weekend

Call mom 3x per week

Go on 3 dates

Read 2 books on leadership

Workout 5x per week

Create a pitch deck for my start-up idea

Join the board of a nonprofit

Research 5 grad school programs

Decide on location for family vacation

Visit the dentist

Volunteer once a week

Mentor someone at work

Apply to 3 new jobs

Paint the bedroom

Buy a bin to start composting

Cook dinner at home 2x per week

Plan date night 2x per month

Go to one concert

Spend $5 less on food every day

Write a book proposal

Clean out closets

Plant 5 flowers in the garden

Start a gratitude practice 3x per week

Write a journal entry every morning

Host a dinner party

It is now time to set goals! The next step is to go through each of the focus areas that you chose to prioritize and create three to four goals in each one. In the end, you will specify roughly ten to fifteen goals for the next three months. This may seem like a lot, but these will be bite-sized goals that fit within your schedule. As you create your goals, here are six things to keep in mind to guide you:

1. Make goals measurable

2. Break down and sequence goals appropriately

3. "Shoulds" also deserve goals

4. Identify tasks that can be delegated or outsourced

5. Be specific

6. Focus on the how as much as the what

1. Make Goals Measurable

It's important that each of your goals be measurable and actionable. This is how you know when you have accomplished a goal! That means any goal should be very specific and based on an action you are going to take. By setting goals that reflect or embody your dream words, they will ideally guide you toward how you want to feel, but the goals themselves should be concrete.

Also avoid using words that are hard to quantify, like "more" or "less." Use numbers instead. Rather than writing "I am going to write more," phrase your goal like this: "I am going to write for thirty minutes every night." This will also help you create a plan and schedule to accomplish your goals. A good test for whether you are setting attainable goals is if it is something you can put in your calendar. Scheduling your goals will help you understand exactly how much time you need to complete them.

For example, one goal might be to feel more connected to your partner or to feel more confident at work. But "connected" and "confident" describe feelings. Instead, specify things you can do that will hopefully foster or embody those emotions. To feel closer to someone, name several concrete or measurable actions, such as:

- *Plan 1 weekend away this quarter*
- *Have an at-home date night once a week*
- *Give a thoughtful gift*

Then, at the end of the quarter, review what happened. Did you accomplish every goal, and did it improve things in the way you wanted? Then recalibrate or set new goals for the next quarter. This may seem calculated for such an emotional goal, but taking these steps shows that you value this area of your life. Setting goals will lead to the feeling you desire.

As for the other example above, gaining more confidence at work, analyze why you feel this way. Does it stem from internal or external factors? If it's internal, think about what you can do that would increase your confidence. In this case, your goals might be:

- *Spend an extra 15 minutes preparing before important meetings*
- *Make at least 1 suggestion at every meeting this quarter*
- *Meet with your boss to check in once a week*

If your lack of confidence stems from external sources, such as an unsupportive boss or culture, you would identify different actions. This doesn't mean that your goal would necessarily be to find a new job. It could be, but that's a big leap. First, you could name smaller goals and see if they help improve the situation, such as:

- *Meet with your manager to discuss changing your role*
- *Meet with 3 different departments in your company to learn more about what they do*
- *Spend 1 hour each week researching new positions in other industries*

If you know you want a new job, then name goals related to a job search, such as:

- *Contact 5 recruiters*
- *Email 5 people in your network who might know of opportunities*
- *Spend 30 minutes a day researching job postings online*

2. Break Down and Sequence Goals Appropriately

It's important to break goals down into sequences of actions, especially if you are adding a new area or activity into your life. People often focus on the endgame—"I want to run a marathon" or "I want to write a screenplay"—but as goals, these can be both intimidating and unrealistic depending on your current abilities. Both can undermine our intentions.

Always start at the beginning. For one quarter, make your goal to run for thirty minutes every day, and then the next quarter increase this amount, and in the third quarter, register for a 10K run. Work your way up to your biggest goal. Who knows, you may realize running is not for you! If so, then it's a good thing you didn't waste an entire year feeling like you failed just because you didn't run a marathon.

Writing a film script is an equally challenging goal, so approach it in stages. For one quarter, maybe set these goals:

- *Write for 1 hour every day*
- *Watch 5 films that inspire you*
- *Attend a screenplay-writing workshop*

You may be interested in taking on a new skill or learning a new subject. If you want to learn to play tennis, perhaps list these goals:

- *Identify 5 tennis instructors*
- *Research the instructors through reviews and past clients*
- *Choose one and sign up for the first session*

With practice, you'll figure out what makes for achievable goals within a three-month period. Sometimes, you might set goals that are too easy, and sometimes they might be too hard. That's okay. Doing something is better than saying, "I'd love to learn to play tennis one day," and then never doing anything about it. Over time, tackling bite-sized goals in the right sequence will lead to big accomplishments.

3. "Shoulds" Also Deserve Goals

While we wish we could all spend our time focusing only on what we love, responsibilities are important. So set goals to be as effective and efficient with those responsibilities as possible, so they won't clutter your mind and even worse waste your time. If you have a low-rated focus area that is more of a responsibility, this area can improve with some order and focus. Do this for one quarter and you'll have more freedom to focus on other areas next quarter.

An area that often needs improvement is finances. Sometimes it's necessary to set goals to get your finances organized to move closer to your dream words. After we got married, Nick and I needed to do this, so that quarter my goals in that focus area were as follows:

- *Gather information about all our accounts in one place*
- *Set a monthly budget*
- *Check in on our finances once a month*

If finances are an area of focus, your quarterly goals could be:

- *Set a budget*
- *Identify 5 ways to increase income or cut costs*
- *Enact 2 of those approaches (to either increase income or cut costs)*

Another area that can be a combined must/should for many people is family time. If our job takes away from family time, it can be easy to feel guilty about not doing enough (as well as not meeting the expectations of others). Setting concrete goals can improve this area, but remember, the quality of your time together is as important as the quantity. Consider ways to spend more time as well as ways to make more of the time you have. If there's a particular family member you'd like to spend more time with, set a goal to see them a certain number of times a week or a month.

While it can't be a goal every quarter, planning a yearly family vacation is a good way to maximize quality time. Even taking a weekend away when everyone can truly be present can be more valuable than a number of casual evenings when everyone is distracted.

The goals for one quarter could simply be related to planning an annual family vacation:

- *Research 8 places to go on vacation*
- *Narrow down locations to a list of 3*
- *Choose a destination and date with the rest of the family*

4. Identify Tasks That Can Be Delegated or Outsourced

As I discuss in "Getting the Highest Return on Investment" (page 144), we can't do everything, and some tasks are better delegated to others or outsourced to professionals. Hiring others to accomplish what we want counts as a goal! For instance, redecorating your home or painting your bedroom might bring you closer to your dream word *home*, but is painting your bedroom yourself the best use of your time? Maybe, if it brings you a sense of fulfillment, but this is the perfect kind of task to outsource. Other goals could be enlisting a babysitter, organizing child care, or hiring housecleaners. Getting this support, even on a temporary basis, can free up time you can use in following quarters for other priorities.

If you don't have the money in your budget to hire the help you need, then your goals for the quarter might include budgeting and saving to afford outsourcing in future quarters.

Or the goals might simply be finding an interior decorator to hire:

- *Ask 4 friends for decorator recommendations*
- *Interview 2 potential decorators*
- *Hire a decorator*

If you're doing the work yourself, then your goals can be more specific:

- *Buy furniture for living room and dining room*
- *Decide on sofa in family room*
- *Install new lighting in the kitchen*

5. Be Specific

Sometimes our focus areas are very generalized, and we need to be more specific to create actionable goals. "More time with friends" is a good example. If this is your focus area for one quarter, write down exactly which friends you want to spend more time with and exactly how often you want to see them. This fosters a proactive approach to life. These goals might be as follows:

- *Meet Anita for coffee once a week*
- *Have a phone chat with Anjula once a month*
- *Plan a weekend away with Shivika and Melanie*

This kind of specific planning is also important in other areas like self-care. There are many ways you can invest in yourself. It's so vast that sometimes it's hard to even know where to start.

So write down three or four ways that are accessible and fit your life that quarter:

- *Go to yoga on Saturdays*
- *Meditate once a week*
- *Journal before bedtime 3 times a week*
- *Get a massage*

It can be easy to forgo self-care, which often feels like a personal luxury, when other things come up. But if we prioritize self-care in our quarterly goals, it becomes something we have to get done. Don't make anything optional if it's important to you. Change your mindset and make it happen.

6. Focus on the How as Much as the What

To be specific and measurable, many goals focus on the outcome, such as "Cook dinner three nights each week," or "Grow social media followers to X." This is good, but it's also important to think about the steps needed to reach that outcome and about your own personal skills and experience. Design your goals so they specify how you will achieve what you want, in part based on your unique abilities and experiences.

For instance, are you familiar with the task or is the goal something new that you are trying for the first time? If you are new to cooking, then your goal to cook three times a week will involve a steeper learning curve than for someone who is familiar in the kitchen. If cooking is a new skill, break down the goal into smaller steps, such as:

- *Browse and choose 3 recipes every Sunday*
- *Grocery shop for all meal ingredients on Monday*
- *Cook 3 meals from Tuesday to Saturday*

Similarly, in your goals, specify how you will grow your social media following. In fact, you might use the goals in one quarter to develop a strategy (by talking to friends and doing research), and the goals of the next quarter could focus on creating content:

- *Find a videographer*
- *Schedule dates for 2 shoots*
- *Edit the content*
- *Post 2 pieces of content*

In other words, use goal setting to plan and strategize the execution of what you want to achieve, and keep goals small and achievable. Remember, the better you get at the small stuff, the less daunting the bigger goals will be. Most importantly, make a plan to move forward.

Create the Plan

With those six guidelines in mind, write down three to four goals for each of the four to five focus areas you chose.

Remember to make these goals reasonable tasks that you can accomplish over the next three months. Once you've written down your goals, go through each one and visualize yourself doing each of them. Take your time with this.

Ideally, as you picture yourself accomplishing each goal, you should feel excited about it. If a particular goal doesn't excite you right now, then get rid of it and replace it with something else. Perhaps make a note to reconsider that goal the next quarter. Your intuition is telling you that now is not the right time for this particular goal, even if the reason for your reaction is unclear.

Using this method has taught me to listen to this inner voice and to let my emotions drive me as much as my intellect and ability to get things done. These are important and overlooked skills.

Finally, consider all the goals you've written down in total, and think about how you'll feel in three months after you've completed them all. If this seems overwhelming or stressful, go back and revise your goals into smaller, less daunting steps. Ideally, you'll be super motivated and passionate about diving in. Remember, this is not a to-do list. Rather, you have made a plan to take full control of your life and to start living passionately and to your full potential.

It's important to also give thought to how you will execute this process in an ongoing fashion, and later in this chapter, I provide more advice and instruction for executing this plan over the next three months and beyond. It's one thing to write down your goals and another to actually accomplish them. A week or a few days before the next quarter arrives, draft a new set of goals for the coming three months. To do this, start by reviewing and rating the list of ten to fifteen priorities you already created (see "Focus: What Are Your Priorities?," page 173), and choose three to four focus areas. You can choose the same focus areas as the previous quarter, all new ones, or a combination. Then, as before, name three to four small, measurable goals for each focus area. Depending on how the previous quarter went and the nature of the focus areas, consider setting slightly more challenging goals, so that each quarter you build momentum and progress exponentially.

At the end of the year, start the process over from scratch. Reflect on your year, choose new dream words that you want to define the coming year, and set quarterly goals to move toward all of them.

Payal

REFLECT WORDS

Unpredictable, Lonely, Passionate, Focused, Unhealthy

DREAM WORDS

Leadership, Growth, Strength, Performance (dance), Stability

TIME ANALYSIS

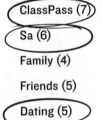

ClassPass (7)

Sa (6)

Family (4)

Friends (5)

Dating (5)

Working Out (7)

Travel (3)

Self-Care (4)

Health (3)

GOALS

ClassPass

· Close seed round
· Launch ClassPass in another city
· Build leadership team of 3

Sa

· Reserve Alvin Ailey Theater
· Set weekly rehearsal schedule for dancers to meet 2x/week
· Cut music for the show
· Choreograph 3 new pieces

Relationships

· Go on 1 date a week
· Ask 3 friends to set me up
· Go out 1x a weekend with friends

Health

· Get an annual physical
· Begin taking iron supplements daily
· Eat a healthy dinner 3x week

Work out

· Run 3x week
· Dance cardio 2x week
· Try a new class 2x week

Set Goals: My Story

With my dream words for the next year on the top of my mind and my focus areas identified, it was finally time to figure out my plan. I wrote down goals that specified changes to my team as well as fundraising and growth targets for ClassPass. I decided to produce a show at the same theater I had booked years earlier to put on another weekend-long Sa showcase. While this was later in the year, I wanted to begin setting a goal to work toward this performance. I also put a healthier meal plan in place and set a list of doctors' appointments to get a better pulse on my health. With this newfound certainty and specific, measurable goals, I made tremendous progress in each focus area. However, the most life-changing involved relationships.

Knowing that I wanted a relationship with longevity, one goal I made was to spend some time with couples who shared stable, lasting relationships. I saw what made them tick and helped them work. I also started going on more dates, and I approached them with a much more open mind, with the energy of someone who knew what she wanted.

During this quarter, my thirty-first birthday arrived. On my past few birthdays, I'd felt a bit sad about still being single. It seemed like all my friends were married or in relationships. But this time, since I was making progress with my dating goal, I didn't really care. Two of my closest girlfriends came over for a quiet birthday celebration, and then a family friend who lived in my apartment building invited the three of us over for a Super Bowl party. Normally, I would have said no. I was usually too busy working, but it was my birthday, I was feeling good, and we decided to go.

We were watching the game when someone knocked on the door, and Nick walked in. He was handsome, with nice eyes and an infectious smile, and he immediately grabbed my attention. He settled on the other side of the room, but we kept glancing at each other all night. At the end of the game, we finally moved closer and started talking. I never stayed out late, but that night, I hung out at the apartment talking to Nick for a long time. The next day, we connected over Facebook, and he asked me to dinner. Our first date was the following night.

I didn't know this at the time, but after that date, Nick asked some of his married friends, "When you met your wife, did you know right away?" I knew in my gut that things were different this time around, too. We started hanging out every night, and I felt the sense of loyalty and commitment that I'd been looking for. He was as passionate about his work as a lawyer as I was about ClassPass and dance. It was as if, once I'd clearly told the universe what I desired, it provided it exactly in the form of Nick!

The truth is, the first time I set my three-month goals, I didn't refer to them often. But they stayed in the back of my mind, setting the direction for my actions. A few months after, I found the scrap of paper I had written my goals on and realized that I had accomplished everything on my list. Indeed, completing those goals had made me feel like a strong, stable leader and performer, and most of all, my three-month relationship goal had resulted in finding the love of my life.

Who can say for sure what would have happened if I hadn't set these goals? I would have moved forward in my life, but setting my intentions and making plans helped me move forward in ways that, up to then, I had been neglecting. Without my goals, I'm certain that I wouldn't have made changes in these areas

SEEING THE LIFEPASS METHOD IN PRACTICE

Since developing this method, I've had the opportunity to share it with friends, family, employees, and others in my life. In the following pages, you will find examples of how four different people have put the process into practice. These examples come from a diverse array of people—some older, some younger, some first timers and others who have been using the method for several years. In addition to detailing their reflect words, dream words, time analysis, focus areas, and goals, they have each explained where they were when they began the process and their experience since using the method. I wanted to share these real-life goal-setting examples so you can get a sense of the power of this practice. Yet these should serve merely as a guide; your content will reflect your own journey and be inspired by your own potential.

Carolyn French

21, Chronicle Prism editorial intern

I am entering my final year at the University of California, Santa Barbara. I live in a college town with my eight roommates, spending my time working as an editorial intern for Chronicle Books.

A year ago, I tested positive for COVID-19. Everything I had planned for my upcoming year, from my booked flight to study abroad in Denmark to the in-person internship meant to jumpstart my career, had slipped through my fingers. I've spent the past year navigating unpredictability, with a loss in faith in the power of planning. I lost sight of the lifelong goals I aimed to achieve and the adventures that bring joy to my life. Going through the LifePass Method was a wakeup call to the control I possess over my own experiences, something that has felt out of reach given the state of a Corona-centered world.

The dream words I chose were *Adventurous, Purposeful, Healthy, Liberated, Hopeful.* After some reflection on the prior year, I realized that my priorities lay in taking advantage of my youth, preparing myself for graduation and my entrance into the workforce, and reconnecting with what brings me joy. While my education and career are top priorities for me, I recognized that I am living my goals already. I am set to graduate early and am currently working my dream internship with Chronicle Books, and I couldn't be happier with where my hard work has carried me professionally. So I decided to focus my goals toward my personal life. I've set goals to spend more time outdoors, take time for self-care, and build deeper connections with my community. I feel hopeful in letting my weekly goals be a vessel to the adventure I seek, the personal health I need, and the purpose that will guide my future. Long-term visions become manageable with short steps rather than large leaps.

REFLECT WORDS

Adventurous, Anxious, Connection, Independent, Unconventional

DREAM WORDS

Adventurous, Purposeful, Healthy, Liberated, Hopeful

TIME ANALYSIS

Education (6)

Exploring/Travel (6)

Friendships (7)

Romantic relationships (4)

Work (8)

Personal Time/Self-care (6)

Social Media (2)

Reading (6)

Fitness and healthy habits (6)

Music/Guitar and singing (4)

Family (7)

Spending time in the outdoors (6)

Meditation and yoga (4)

GOALS

Spending time in the outdoors

- Jump in the ocean 3 days each week
- Plan 1 night of camping every month
- Hike or run a new trail in Santa Barbara twice a week

Personal Time/Self-care

- Spend 1 hour reading 3 days a week
- Spend 20 minutes meditating 3 days a week
- Spend 10 minutes journaling 3 days a week

Friendships—building a support system

- Get coffee with 1 new person from my community
- Check in with 1 of my housemates 5 days a week and focus on actively listening to them
- Cook 1 of my housemates breakfast once a week

Claire Goodill

*30, head of partnerships for an ecommerce
marketing technology software company*

I've been feeling like the ways I spend my time (i.e., work and parts of my social life) are misaligned with what I want in life. Quite frankly, I was pretty overwhelmed, and even at times sad going into this goal setting, because I was aware I wanted to make changes, but didn't know where to start.

I started the LifePass Method with an awareness that I needed to change course, but overwhelmed on how to do it. I've been using the LifePass Method for a few years now. I'm consistently motivated by the process. Setting goals can sound overwhelming if they're annual goals that are very high level and lack accountability. However, setting very tactical goals, which are written down and shared with those you love, trust, or who push you, is motivating. In fact, it's almost freeing.

One time I did my goals when I was in debt and unhappy with my job. Without this framework, my default would have been to tell myself I needed to save money and job search. In literal terms, those were true statements. Yet what I actually needed to *do* was take action today. What I needed to *do* was switch to a 0 percent interest credit card, and set a payoff schedule that I stuck to. I did it! I also needed to reach out to at least three investors who were investing in companies I was interested in—these turned into interviews! So no, I didn't get a new job or get out of debt the very day I wrote my goals, but I did take the first steps that ultimately got me there very soon after.

I've also found myself consistently making it a goal to journal about a certain topic regularly. Journaling is still not a habit for me, but it's beneficial when I do it, so I made it a goal—specifically to help achieve my dream word *love*. I found myself writing that the small things didn't matter, and that I was really happy about the things that mattered most—which led me to fall deeply for my boyfriend at the time. Now that I've made *love* a dream word, I know that making time to date is aligned with what I want and I shouldn't feel guilty about giving time to this.

Most recently, I've noticed that the entrepreneurial itch I've had for almost a decade is growing. I've pushed this down for ten years, but why? Well, it's likely because I continue to find myself in very fortunate work situations with amazing people. It's hard to leave that behind. However, one of the dream words I set is *entrepreneurship*, so it's now a goal to start building. I'm sharing these goals with my friends and family because I know they'll support me.

REFLECT WORDS
Independent, Adventurous, Insecure, Friendships, Leadership

DREAM WORDS
Love, Health, Wealth, Adventure, Entrepreneurship

TIME ANALYSIS

Health (4)	Cleaning (5)
Reading (6)	Creative work (3)
Work, managing (2)	Family calls (7)
Work, strategy (6)	Quality time with friends (6)
Entrepreneurship (3)	Social media (4)
Love (3)	Wealth (2)
Adventure (6)	

GOALS

Love

- Get a therapist
- Keep a list of everything I like about the guys I'm dating and everything that bothers me. Order each list by importance of what matters most to me
- Spend a weekend away—and not working—with the person I'm interested in

Health

- Cut out all red meat and dairy
- Get my CRP HS-Cardiac tested
- Sleep at least 7 hours a night. To do this, I'll need to go to bed earlier (not sleep in longer). I'm going to try to go to bed by 11:30 every weeknight
- Limit added sugars or allergens when not eating socially
- Figure out my health insurance options for when I'm no longer on my current company's plan

Wealth

- Set a budget for H2. Include a list of current recurring expenses I could cut out or cut down on
- Reach out to 5 prospective financial advisors
- Inquire about employee referral signing bonus for the referral I made to the company I work for

Entrepreneurship

- Conduct 2 hours of competitive research on the femtech industry each week
- Finalize terms with a lawyer
- Have 4 user research calls with former or current surrogates or egg donors

Adventure

- Plan a solo day in Greece to explore
- Create a list of 10 activities or places that would feel out of my comfort zone, yet realistic to visit or do this quarter; pick one or two

Abiman Rajadurai

37, in-house attorney

I wasn't searching for a new way to organize my goals, but I gave the LifePass Method a shot because I constantly assess whether I am maximizing my potential personally, professionally, and in the community. The focus during the latter part of 2020 and the start of 2021 was around surviving. Today, it's time to return to "normal" and focus on thriving. The LifePass Method gave me the flexibility to identify and chase goals during these vastly different phases of my life.

The LifePass Method's focus on achieving particular feelings is markedly different from the traditional approach of solely pinpointing specific measurable goals. The focus on feelings reframes success and has enabled me to feel fulfilled more frequently. Success results from a series of choices that can be repeated on the journey to one's goals as opposed to the isolated moment a goal is attained. The quarterly approach offers me the opportunity to regularly measure and reassess my intentions, goals, and progress while also providing flexibility in the event of unforeseen changes at home or work (even if faced with a global pandemic!). Finally, tying the time–value exercise to feelings helps me more easily eliminate activities that I thought were essential but were actually superfluous. Outside of setting and achieving goals, this process has had the unexpected benefit of helping me lead a more authentic and empowered life. I am able to rapidly assess whether to take on opportunities and events based on whether they align with my focus words and the feelings that I want to experience.

Since starting this process last year, I have had a much easier time allocating my time and budget, accomplished numerous goals, and continue to find new ways to challenge myself. I am looking forward to continuing this process through Q3 2021 and beyond!

REFLECT WORDS

Survive, Uncertain, Solutions, Connection, Growth

DREAM WORDS

Thrive, Challenge, Inspire, Family, Presence

TIME ANALYSIS

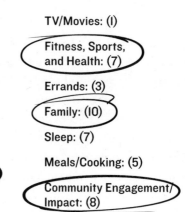

Texting: (I–IO depending on situation/connection)

Sports blogs/news: (2)

Watching live sports: (I–IO quality v. quantity)

Social Media: (2)

Work: (9)

Personal Development: (6)

Reading: (4)

TV/Movies: (I)

Fitness, Sports, and Health: (7)

Errands: (3)

Family: (IO)

Sleep: (7)

Meals/Cooking: (5)

Community Engagement/Impact: (8)

GOALS

Work
- Catch up with 1 legal team member and business team member each week
- Develop goals and action items for cross-functional project
- Create, or volunteer for, at least 1 new stretch assignment/project

Fitness
- Complete both Peloton Power Zone Courses as well as Core Program
- Score 145 or higher on FTP (Functional Threshold Power) test
- Take a tennis class 1x/week and either lesson/ball machine/match 1x/week

Family
- Have 2 phone-free weeknights per week and have more focused weekend plans
- Plan August family vacation
- Go on 1 date night per week

Community Engagement/Impact
- Develop and execute second annual summer Instagram fundraiser
- Prepare and present fundraising proposal for Board Development Committee
- Meet 1:1 with 2 members of each board

Personal Development
- Prepare and present Capstone Project for SABA Leadership Institute
- Identify next leadership/management/strategy program
- Read 8–10 books

Carmina Diaz

26, account coordinator at a publicity firm

Before being introduced to the LifePass Method I was always on the go but never really going anywhere. There was always a feeling of uncertainty in what I was doing.

Having come across the LifePass Method has not only helped me organize the way I go about achieving my dreams, but it made me realize that I was placing myself second to everyone else and that I hadn't been giving myself the attention and time I needed to grow. Part of this is because I'm a people pleaser and have trouble saying no. With the LifePass Method, I have learned to reevaluate my priorities and have come to the realization that it's okay to be "selfish" with my time—especially when it comes to my dreams and ambitions. With this process you learn to organize your thoughts and actions as well as how to manage your time and how to spend it wisely.

This method has given me the flexibility to constantly reassess and pivot my approach on completing my goals by also taking into account my feelings. Before, I would put my feelings aside and tackle any activity that would bring me one step closer to my end goal, but this would often result in me giving up as I would lose interest. This process has helped me reevaluate and reflect on whether the goals I have set for myself are something I really want to do and if my approach is the right way to go about it. LifePass has really helped me become more organized in all aspects of my life—beyond my goals. I'm happy with the results I've been seeing. Before, I felt stagnant and lost, but now I can actually see my progress and I'm excited for what's to come.

REFLECT WORDS

Uncertainty, Stagnant, Family, Secure, Independent

DREAM WORDS

Purposeful, Healthy, Creative, Wealth, Travel

TIME ANALYSIS

Family (7)

Friends (8)

Health (10)

Finances (10)

Work (8)

Romance (3)

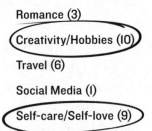

Creativity/Hobbies (10)

Travel (6)

Social Media (1)

Self-care/Self-love (9)

GOALS

Health (overall)

- Schedule a physical
- Do at least 30 minutes of physical activity every day
- Cook at least 3 healthy meals a week

Finances

- Track spending habits
- Set monthly allowance of $500 for food, drinks, miscellaneous purchases
- Meet with financial advisor

Friends

- Check in with friends weekly
- Go out at least once a month with friends
- Share my feelings more with Stephanie

Hobbies

- Buy roller skates
- Practice being on roller skates
- Go to the roller rink

Self-care/Self-love

- Go to dermatologist to start a self-care skin routine
- Find a therapist

EXECUTE

What's your potential?

In the years since I developed the LifePass Method, this goal-setting tool has helped me push my life in new directions, reconnect to my why during times of confusion and crisis, and evolve as a human being, both personally and professionally. My dream words act as a constant reminder throughout the year of what is important to me so I never veer too far off course. Revisiting my focus areas and goals each quarter gives me an opportunity to keep experimenting with new passions, pushing harder, and dreaming bigger.

I've managed to accomplish my goals and dreams since starting this process—from finding a life partner, raising a toddler, and traveling the world to cultivating a billion-dollar idea, building a national dance company, and advising and investing in other incredible creatives and founders! I keep all my goals in one place so I can track my progress over the years and see what things I've decided to push further into and what I've let go of. For example, after years of dreaming, I have finally begun training again in a form of classical Indian dance called Kathak, which I have been enjoying immensely. At the same time, I tried to take on cooking and have just not found enough personal momentum—thank goodness for my husband and Uber Eats!

My hope is that this method can do the same for you. But it doesn't happen overnight. By starting small and setting new goals each quarter, you will gain confidence as you meet goal after goal. Over time, you'll naturally start to set bigger and bolder goals that will help you evolve in all areas of your life.

One of my favorite aspects of this process is that every quarter is a fresh chance to try something new and take a slightly bigger leap. Those leaps build on one another so that by the time you're finally ready to take a huge leap, it will feel like just another step you are ready to conquer.

Throughout this chapter, I provide advice for accomplishing the goals you've set and executing the plan you've made over the course of the three months. These strategies will help keep you on track even as life throws you curveballs. Ultimately, as you succeed at your goals, even if they are small steps, this builds confidence, so that with each new three-month period, you learn how much you can accomplish and how much more you can challenge yourself.

Successful execution often involves these six approaches:

1. Schedule your goals

2. Learn to say no

3. Check in with your progress

4. Be accountable to your goals

5. Share your goals

6. Keep your dream words close

I. Schedule Your Goals

The first approach is to translate each of your goals into time. Next to each goal on your list, allocate the approximate number of hours per day, week, or month that you are going to spend on this item. Obviously, each goal will be different, and some goals will require more time than others. Be realistic about the amount of time it will take to get each one done, but also, don't allocate more time than you think you can give. Set yourself up for success by setting reasonable expectations. If, while doing this, you find a goal will clearly require more time than you have, revise the goal. Then, at the end of the quarter, if you feel you could have accomplished more, you can take on a bigger challenge next quarter.

Once you decide how much time you are going to dedicate to each goal, schedule it into your calendar, so the time you need to execute is blocked out. For example, if your goal is to spend more time with three friends or mentors, contact them to plan and schedule each get-together. If you set a goal to explore a new hobby, decide how much time you can devote to it and how often. If you decide to commit to one hour each week, set aside that hour in your calendar ahead of time. Even though the time may shift, it's easier to move things around than create new pockets of time!

Remember, you have an entire quarter to achieve your goals, which allows you to space things out over three months. Don't expect to get everything done in a single day, week, or even month. During some weeks, one goal will get more time than others. At other times, something more pressing might force you to set aside all your goals; when this happens, try to reschedule your goals within what remains of the quarter. The benefit of scheduling your goals weeks or months in advance is that then you know you've planned for completing all your priorities and giving them the time they need. This helps avoid any stress or worry over not doing everything right away.

Achieving goals is a step-by-step process—one step leads to the next. If you try to do it all at once, you won't be able to give each goal your all and do them all well. Map out the steps and start walking, and soon you'll be climbing the highest mountains.

2. Learn to Say No

The goal-setting method in this book is about saying yes to what we want. I believe that if we focus on the things we want to spend time doing, then this naturally results in spending less time on things we don't enjoy or that don't support our dreams. A life of yes is much better than a life of no, and by focusing on our goals, other things tend to end up in the appropriate place. That said, sometimes we do need to say no. Just as importantly, when we do, we shouldn't feel bad for it.

Through this goal-setting process, we identify what we want our priorities to be (at least for each quarter), and we commit to fulfilling the goals we set. In itself, this isn't selfish; it's how we foster our best selves, by prioritizing what we love. Of course, we will encounter conflicts with our time, and to complete our goals, we might have to say no to others—to socializing, family events, work outings, coffee dates, and so on. We might have to change our routine in ways others don't like. We might wish we had more hours or didn't have to say no, but we've identified something important that deserves our attention: our purpose and mission.

When you have to say no, explain why (if that's appropriate), but don't feel guilty. Guilt wastes valuable time and won't help you move forward toward your goals. However, if you find that you say no more often than *you* want, and you are neglecting things that are important to *you*, consider these things against your dream words and then use this information to revise your goals and priorities next quarter.

3. Check In with Your Progress

Either weekly or at some other regular interval, review your goals and keep track of how you're progressing. Don't wait until the end of three months to see how you did. Make sure you are keeping up with what you've scheduled, then plan ahead while keeping your goals in mind.

As I describe (see "The Art of Scheduling," page 140), I have a Sunday-night ritual of reviewing my goals and setting my schedule for the coming week, and I recommend that you create a similar regular check-in that fits your life. This allows you to recalibrate your schedule and expectations as you go and make adjustments. For instance, if something doesn't get done when you thought it would, you can schedule it for the next week. Or if you know the coming week will be too busy to fit the goals you have planned, you can put those goals off and do them the following week. This keeps you from falling behind or overlooking something.

In moments when you find yourself stressed out, busy, or even needing to make hard choices about your time, turn to your goals to serve as a guide and reminder of what's most important. Your plan was set with intention and clarity, and revisiting it will help you remember what matters most. It can be all too easy to let other people's priorities overshadow your own, and so returning to and keeping regular track of your goals is one way to avoid that from happening.

4. Be Accountable to Your Goals

Ultimately, success with anything in life is dependent on our level of motivation. This method is designed to build motivation by identifying goals that we *want* to prioritize. However, we are the only ones who can hold ourselves accountable for following through. Self-awareness here is key. Are you someone who is typically self-motivated, or are you someone who does better with an external source driving you? If the latter, what has worked for you in the past?

Many people prefer when someone else helps hold them accountable. If that's you, consider whether you have a friend or partner who can serve in this role. If so, the best approach is to do the goal-setting method together, so you can both promise to hold each other accountable. Another method that works well is establishing a way to celebrate the completion of every single goal, or even when making measurable progress on a goal. What type of reward or acknowledgment might help keep you motivated through the ups and downs?

Finally, the point is for this method to become a way of life where our priorities matter. In itself, this experience and sense of fulfillment often fosters discipline. At first, however, to keep yourself moving forward and hitting your goals, it never hurts to do whatever you can to hold yourself accountable as you go. The more you taste living life on your terms, the hungrier you'll be for more.

5. Share Your Goals

Even if you are self-motivated and don't need help from anyone else to stay on track, I still recommend sharing your goals with the important people in your life. When the people we love know what is most important to us, they are so much more likely to invest in our success. Not only will they want to help in any practical ways they can, but they will also be less likely to encourage or pressure us to spend our time on other things. They will understand why we have to say no to certain invitations or obligations, and they might even go out of their way to help us protect our time so we can focus on our goals.

Many people are scared to share their passions with the people closest to them. I understand this instinct. It is an emotional risk to put our deepest desires out into the world. Sometimes, we might feel like we are disappointing people if our definition of success is not aligned with theirs. Nevertheless, the point of this method is to live by our own terms. Keeping our goals from the people who care about us deprives them of an opportunity to help us succeed.

Take a moment to write down a list of the people you are going to share your goals with. This should include anyone you would include on your Team Life, and anyone who might be affected by your changing priorities or who might help you achieve your goals—such as by sharing resources, offering support, or providing opportunities. Simply having other people rooting for you is incredibly motivating.

6. Keep Your Dream Words Close

Finally, as you move forward, keep your dream words close so you are always in tune with why you are doing all of this. If you want, post your words somewhere you will see them every day, or meditate on them as part of a daily practice. When decisions and opportunities and outside pressures come up, weigh them against your dream words. Would saying yes to this opportunity lead you in the direction of your words or not? If the answer is no, why would you say yes when you could be putting that time toward something that would move you instead in the right direction? These words are your true north for the year. Let them guide you toward your potential.

REVIEW YOUR GOALS AND EVALUATE YOUR SUCCESS

After the first quarter, check in and evaluate how you did on your first round of goals. Did you do what you set out to do? Even when everything goes well, we don't always accomplish all of our goals.

First, think about any goals you didn't reach. What stood in your way? Was it a mental obstacle like fear or doubt, a lack of execution, or a practical constraint? Consider the goal itself. Perhaps it simply wasn't the right time. In this case, set this goal aside, knowing you can get back to it when the time is right. Was the goal too big and ambitious to accomplish in one quarter? If so, use this valuable information when planning for the next quarter and create smaller goals. It's better to set modest goals we can accomplish than to set huge goals and feel like we've failed or were too scared to get started.

Consider the goals you did accomplish. What helped you succeed, and how did it feel? Did reaching these goals help you move closer to your dream words? Did this feel the way you expected it to or not? If you accomplished a goal and want to continue with this effort—maybe you uncovered something exciting to advance it in new ways—then keep it as a goal next quarter. I often do that! Or perhaps there was something you thought you wanted that didn't end up being right for you. Be honest with yourself. Sometimes the things we think will make us happy don't end up delivering the way we expect them to. This can feel disappointing, but it is not a failure; it's information. Recognize this and adjust your goals rather than continuing down the wrong path.

If you accomplished a goal and it didn't feel the way you expected it to, is this because it was the wrong goal or because your dream words didn't end up feeling authentic to you after all? Normally, I recommend keeping the same dream words for a full year, but if you realize that the ones you have are not right for you, feel free to choose new ones that feel more authentic. If, however, the dream words still feel right but the goal itself did not move you closer to them, consider this a success. For example, maybe you tried to learn a new skill but found it unfulfilling. That's okay! Not everything is going to work out. You still reached your goal and you learned something important about yourself. That's a great place from which to start setting new goals.

Before letting go of a goal, just check in and make sure you're doing so for the right reasons—not because of doubt or fear, but because it is not serving you in the way you truly want. If you're not sure, think about the opportunity cost of continuing to pursue this goal. Is there something you'd rather be doing with this time? If so, you can move on with confidence. If not, try to pinpoint what held you back from passionately chasing this goal and working through that constraint, and then try again. I often recalibrate goals or even throw them out completely. While the goals may change, the true north embodied by our dream words stays the same.

EXPECT THE UNEXPECTED

Despite setting small, attainable goals and creating a solid plan for execution, we very often encounter unexpected obstacles that keep us from succeeding. After all, no one can control the future, and unforeseen events can ruin the best-laid plans. The most dramatic example of this is the Covid-19 pandemic, which in spring 2020 upended life for everyone across the globe.

Whether events are large or small, if something out of your control happens that stops you from executing your goals as planned, adjust your goals so you can keep moving forward in any possible way. The easiest way to do this is to set another goal in the same focus area. For instance, if you set a new fitness goal and suffer an injury, you might shift to taking low-impact classes that assist with your recovery. During the pandemic, ClassPass shifted to a digital strategy to keep people moving, people who ran restaurants created outdoor seating and featured food delivery, and people who ran retail stores shifted to online shopping. The key is to keep moving toward where you want to go.

If it's not possible to set a new goal in the same focus area, pick a new focus area and set a new goal to work toward in the remaining time in that quarter. View these shifts as opportunities, not failures. When life forces us to change our plans and goals, that's not our fault, but we can set new goals and work toward them, while still moving forward in the direction of our dream words. For example, if an injury makes all exercise impossible, consider creating a new relationship goal that you can accomplish as your body recovers. This could be increasing time with children or friends.

As you repeat the LifePass Method over time, you will become more in tune with what you want out of your life, what emotions you want to feel, and what actions will help you get there. At the same time, you'll get better about prioritizing and focusing your time and executing your plans. The more you repeat this process, the more intuitive it will become.

AFTERWORD

WE OFTEN HEAR "the only constant is change." This is true in the tech industry and true in our lives. We are constantly in motion. We are constantly evolving, and that means that every day we have an opportunity to become an even better version of ourselves.

Companies always pivot and innovate. As humans we can and must do the same to keep moving forward to reach our highest potential. The most influential people in history all had to change paths many times to be able to reach the transforming places they did. The journey and path may not always be laid out in front of us—and if we're truly following our unique calling, it most likely won't be. This requires choosing a direction, moving forward, reassessing our progress, and making the conscious decision to evolve and grow.

Someone a few years back asked me a question that threw me off guard. I was asked: "Payal, how does it feel that you'll never do anything as big as ClassPass again in your life?"

It took me a minute to feel the weight of that thought—the idea that my future might pale in comparison to what I had done in the past and that my greatest career highs might be over.

This question brought up a lot of anxiety during the pandemic and especially as the discussions of ClassPass being acquired by Mindbody took center stage. I finally found some silence and stillness to really hear my thoughts and even my fears. As I spent more time with my young son, I found myself wondering: *Who is the woman and mama my son is going to see while he is growing up?* I was no longer the old me: the person I was before he was born, before I got married, before I started ClassPass. I had been through a lot in ten years, but who was I now and what did I want to be doing?

I started to ask myself the hard questions I raise in this book: *What is my calling? Who am I? What am I scared of? Whose life am I living? What is holding me back?*

These questions made me uncomfortable and I questioned myself: *Can I be a great dancer as I approach my forties? Who am I outside of being the founder of ClassPass? Should I start a new company? Am I spending enough time with my son?*

This led me to return to the "shoulds" and identify conflicts that I've wrestled with all my adult life: of being a female entrepreneur and of whether I was an adequate role model for other women and was living up to societal expectations as a wife, mom, and daughter. I knew I couldn't do it all or have it all or be it all—the all that others expect, or the all that we sometimes put on ourselves—because everything we accomplish comes with trade-offs and sacrifices and ups and downs.

I also realized that we never achieve "balance." Instead, the best we can do is learn to adapt and change and be our whole selves in every moment even as our needs and wants and circumstances constantly evolve. This is the message that I aim to convey in this book, and I hope my stories, mantras, and advice help you to name your purpose and go for it no matter what happens along the way. Of course, it's never easy, but it's always worthwhile.

Maybe I won't build another ClassPass—or maybe I will. All I know is that I will continue to identify what I love and strive for that . . . and that is truly all that matters.

As you move forward toward the things that light you up, remember these mantras:

I strive to find and follow my unique purpose in this life.

My differences make me exceptional.

The most important voice to listen to is my own.

Fear and doubt are only in my mind.

I don't work for money; money works for me.

I am capable of doing anything I work hard for.

Who I surround myself with is my decision.

I am the only one in control of my time.

ACKNOWLEDGMENTS

FIRST AND FOREMOST, I WANT TO thank Anita Chatterjee who is the main reason I wrote this book and likely the reason many of you heard about me or LifePass. She believed sharing this story of an Indian American woman would inspire others of all backgrounds, and as my publicist she made sure it would reverberate. She helped push the idea of LifePass further and bigger every step of the process, even in the midst of having her first child.

I also would like to thank the authors and team behind this book.

Jodi Lipper spent time with me in learning about my life and my methodology to further translate them into stories and lessons for the reader. I am appreciative of all her time and help in the creation of this book—especially in the middle of the pandemic!

Carlye Adler joined me in the final months of completing this manuscript to help make it truly come to life. I was so thankful she agreed to add this book to the roster of books that she has written over the years. Carlye was an incredible collaborator, and my time with her writing this book was joyful, therapeutic, and has earned me a new friend for life!

I'm thankful to my literary agent, Mollie Glick, who for years had encouraged me to write a book. I knew when I was ready, there was no one else I'd want to work with given her sharp eye for talent and ability to execute. She helped connect me to our wonderful publisher, Chronicle Prism. I am grateful to everyone there, especially to Cara Bedick, who helped champion this book from the beginning, and to Brooke Johnson and Gabriele Wilson for the beautiful design.

This book and its concepts come from my life, which has been deeply impacted by those around me. My mom and dad have been my number-one cheerleaders from the beginning, setting me up to have a platform to leap from. My sister, Avani, provided me with a great role model to look up to my entire life. My dance teacher, Usha Patel, taught me how to succeed in life, which is a big part of what I share in this book. My husband, Nick, has been a constant supporter, from the wording in the book to bringing me the best snacks during my writing and reading days! Also, much love to my brother-in-law Arjun Patel, my nephews Keeran and Ishan Patel, and the entire Pujji family for filling my life with such joy.

I wrote this book in the middle of the pandemic. Six weeks before it started, I gave birth to my beautiful baby boy, Zayn! He has filled our home with so much love and light and taught me many more lessons about life!

Thank you to the beautiful ladies of the Sa Dance Company who went along with my crazy visions and let me become an entrepreneur at such a young age. I would have never seen the potential in myself without the opportunity they all gave me to lead them, teach them, and create with them, which served as the basis to my ClassPass journey.

I am deeply thankful to the ClassPass team. Those who took a bet on the idea and invested in the company and especially those who decided to take a job working on this incredible mission. I have learned so much from each and every one of you, especially my partner, Fritz Lanman, who believed in me from the beginning and has worked endlessly on making our vision come to life. I also want to thank the OG ClassPass team for sticking it through some of our most challenging times: Sanjiv Sanghavi, Rashi Birla, Shiloh Goodin, Cat Stefanovici, Naman Desai, and Atul Ohri.

A big thank-you to some of the mentors, teachers, and advisors who have impacted my life: Anjula Acharia, Andrew Weinrich, Cory Greenberg, Cyrus Massoumi, Cathy Angelastro, Patricia Whitcas, Adam Valkin, David Tisch, Shakil Khan, Daniel Ek, Bhairavi Kumar, Rohan Sheth, Mira Nair, Alexei Cowett, Michael Fleisher, Roger Gold, Stephen Hendel, Margaret Selby, Janina Gavankar, Pooja Narang, Christine Yeh, Seline Karakaya, and Enzo Arena.

Thank you to all my friends and family who have spent time reading the book and sending me thoughts. Big thanks to: Jasmine Weiner, Jay Shetty, Sonia Mukerji, Katie Benner, Zach Apter, Shivika Sahdev, Raakhi Kapur, Raj Brinder Singh, Parul Deora Somani, Samata Narra, Jeremy Skaller, Sandy Pujji, Jesse Pujji, Alex Pujji, and Prerna Gupta.

Special thank you to Abiman Rajadurai, Claire Goodill, Carmina Diaz, and Carolyn French for sharing their stories.

ABOUT THE AUTHOR

PAYAL KADAKIA is the founder of revolutionary fitness and wellness platform, ClassPass, which provides people access to the best boutique fitness classes, gyms, and wellness experiences around the world. Payal is an accomplished dancer and the founder and artistic director of the Sa Dance Company, dedicated to expressing Indian American identity. Payal is frequently featured in major news outlets and has been listed among *Fast Company*'s 100 Most Creative People, and was named to *Fortune*'s 40 under 40 list. She holds a bachelor of science from MIT.